Critical Condition

Critical Condition

Replacing Critical Thinking with Creativity

Patrick Finn

WILFRID LAURIER UNIVERSITY PRESS

Wilfrid Laurier University Press acknowledges the support of the Canada Council for the Arts for our publishing program. We acknowledge the financial support of the Government of Canada through the Canada Book Fund for our publishing activities. This work was supported by the Research Support Fund.

 Canada Council for the Arts   Conseil des Arts du Canada

Library and Archives Canada Cataloguing in Publication

Finn, Patrick, 1966–, author
   Critical condition : replacing critical thinking with creativity / Patrick Finn.

Includes bibliographical references and index.
Issued in print and electronic formats.
ISBN 978-1-77112-157-6 (pbk.).—ISBN 978-1-77112-159-0 (epub).—
ISBN 978-1-77112-158-3 (pdf)

   1. Creative thinking—Study and teaching (Higher). 2. Critical thinking—Study and teaching (Higher). 3. Thought and thinking—Study and teaching (Higher). 4. Creative thinking. 5. Critical thinking. 6. Thought and thinking. I. Title.

LB2395.35.F56 2015   370.15   C2015-901595-2
                                                             C2015-901596-0

Cover design by David Drummond. Text design by Mike Bechthold.

This book is printed on FSC® certified recycled paper and is certified Ecologo. It is made from 100% post-consumer fibre, is processed chlorine free, and is manufactured using biogas energy.

Printed in Canada

Every reasonable effort has been made to acquire permission for copyright material used in this text, and to acknowledge all such indebtedness accurately. Any errors and omissions called to the publisher's attention will be corrected in future printings.

RECYCLED
Paper made from
recycled material
FSC
www.fsc.org   FSC® C103567

Dedication

For my students – thank you.

Contents

Acknowledgements

This little book has had a long journey to print. Along the way it has benefited from a lot of support. Given its quirky nature, I want to begin by explicitly excusing those I am thanking from responsibility for the outlandish things I say below. Those I need to thank are responsible for inspiring and supporting me but should be let off the hook for the rest.

Everything I do academically requires a thank-you to Kathryn Kerby-Fulton and Aritha van Herk. They are the two scholars most responsible for my graduate education and academic career. My parents were also lifelong supporters of my commitment to this path. Two editors have been particularly wonderful – the first, Siobhan McMenemy, was the first person I worked with on this manuscript, and the second, Lisa Quinn, is responsible for bringing it to fruition. Thanks also to the anonymous readers at the press who helped so much in clarifying my thoughts throughout. I am also indebted to my research assistant, Brittany Reid.

I have had many inspiring mentors who have shared my interest in the ideas in this book. Among the most important are Donna Livingstone, Judy Lawrence, Judy McLachlan, Douglas McCullough, Brian Smith, Jay Ingram, Arnie Keller, and Edward Pechter. Special thanks must also go to Melissa Monteros and Wojciech Mochniej for their creative collaboration and to Allan Bell for the same, but also for his "greybeard" advice.

From the time I first came to the University of Calgary I have been very fortunate to be surrounded by wonderful colleagues, staff, and students. I am profoundly grateful to the university and most of all to Clem Martini. Clem was one of the biggest reasons I wanted to come to U of C. He ended up being the Head of Drama when I was a student and again later when I became a faculty member. He remains one of my favourite writers and is now a cherished colleague.

Finally, I want to thank Julie Funk and Molly and Max Finn. It is our families who sacrifice most when we commit to academic work. I could not have written this book without them and I am profoundly grateful to them for their patience and support.

An Invitation

Out beyond ideas of wrongdoing and rightdoing,
there is a field. I'll meet you there.

– Rumi

This short book is an invitation to participate in a thought experiment. I ask you to join me in considering what would happen if we replaced critical thinking with creative practice at the heart of learning. In pursuing this experiment, we will examine some of the history of critical thinking and look at examples of how critical and creative work might operate in the university.

Given that universities are where we train teachers, doctors, lawyers, dancers, politicians, and so many others who influence the way our world works, it seems to me that *how* we do our work matters a great deal. For generations, our accepted practice has been to have every course in the university operate in a mode that foregrounds critical thinking. What would happen if we changed that?

We promise students who arrive on campus that we will turn them into critical thinkers and then go to great lengths to explain that this is a good thing. But is it? Is it good for us? Is it good for everyone? Perhaps it is, but it has been a long time since anyone asked whether critical thinking is helping us. (Actually, it may be that no one has ever asked.) What if it is not? What if it is time we put another way of working at the heart of what we do? And what if that mode is more creative than critical? Why don't we think about this for the next few pages and then have a discussion?

Before we begin we need to address four important elements:

1. We need to define what we mean by critical thinking.
2. We need to note that we are *not* talking about critical theory or criticism.
3. We need to define what we mean by creativity.
4. We need to define what "interdisciplinary" means when it comes to the discussion of the audience for this book.

When we turn to dictionary definitions of critical thinking we find two positive ones and an avalanche of negative ones. "Critical" can mean *important,* as in "let's focus on the critical issues," or it can relate to *reasoned examination,* as in "after critical deliberation ..." Those two definitions allude to what we hope to find in the best of critical thinking. This book asks whether those definitions have ceded their proper place to other definitions. In most dictionary entries, we find words like *disapproving, judgmental,* and *attack.* When we turn to books such as William Hughes's *Critical Thinking: An Introduction to the Basic Skills,* we find commonplaces. Introductions to critical thinking always point out that what the reader *thinks* is critical thinking actually is not. We are told that when we hear the word critical we think of it as negative, when it is not. In books like Hughes's, and in others such as the *Bolinda Introduction to Critical Thinking,* we are told that critical thinking is about something other than what we think. The idea behind this book is that if most people think of being critical as being negative, then perhaps we should ask if there is some truth to the assertion. The reasoning discussed in *Bolinda* and by Hughes is no doubt valuable, but it is not what is commonly known as critical thinking. In fact, *Bolinda* and many others like it are not introductions to critical thinking but rather general introductions to logic. Without question, studying logic would benefit students, but we might ask whether we should not turn to logicians for this instruction rather than farming it out to non-specialists who teach it by another name.

When I talk about critical thinking I often hear passionate arguments about the importance of critical theory. But this book is not directly concerned with critical theory. What I am actually talking about is critical *thinking* – a mode of thinking that is governed by a critical approach to all incoming information that has winners and losers. Critical theory was developed by the Frankfurt School in the 1920s as a method for critiquing various forms of fascism, capitalism, and other structures of power. It is a far more focused mode of intellectual engagement inspired by Marxist thought. Almost every program at every school advocates critical thinking; the commitment to critical theory is decidedly more narrow. So this book is about the influence of critical *thinking*, not the merits of critical *theory*.

There is a mountain of literature about creativity, all of which makes two basic assertions: creativity involves the creation of something *new* that has *value*. This seems simple enough, but what qualifies as *new*? And what counts as having *value*? Here it becomes quite complicated. All creators work from sources, so newness is a matter of degree. Moreover, new does not necessarily signify creative. Our society's incessant drive for the new means that much is created that is new merely for the sake of being new. *Value* is an equally fraught term. The value of creative works is addressed in philosophy by aesthetics and in the economy by the market. For our purposes, creativity requires a mixture of newness and value, but the definitions of those terms are up for discussion. Shakespeare based *Hamlet* on a number of other plays that contained all of the important elements of the story, yet his version was regarded as *new enough* to complement its sources. People have been discussing and debating that play's value for more than four hundred years. Thus, if we were to discuss creativity we could point to *Hamlet* as something that had newness as well as value we can agree upon (though *how much* value remains open for continued examination). An important point when discussing creative thinking is that creativity always involves evaluation. When considering the positive definitions of critical thinking that involve reasoned judgment, we soon realize that any move toward creative thinking involves critical thinking in the evaluative phase.

This book is written for all of my colleagues on campus and for all of those who have an interest in what we do. I take that to be a large number of people, since as noted earlier, universities produce so many of the people who make decisions in our society. When one writes a book for a wide scholarly audience, it is commonly referred to as *interdisciplinary*. To most readers, that word sounds as if it refers to work between disciplines – it seems to promise to fly free of the barriers of disciplinary jargon and method. Unfortunately, like the term critical thinking, its meaning has drifted. A glance at one of the most widely read contributions to the subject is instructive. Joe Moran's *Interdisciplinarity* has five sections. The first focuses on English as a discipline; the second, on literature and culture; the third, on theory and disciplines; the fourth, on texts and history; and the fifth, on science through texts and culture. While taking nothing away from that book, note that interdisciplinary too often means something like "between cognate disciplines that share much of the same language." This book seeks to be *fully* interdisciplinary – to engage people whether they are working in English, engineering, or economics. For that reason, I have tried to keep the language and the examples accessible. I have also included explanatory notes to support further reading for those so inclined.

Chapter I

A Foolish Question

Isn't It Time We Replaced Critical Thinking?

On April Fool's Day of 2011, I stepped out onto the stage of one of the most beautiful buildings in my city. The Grand Theatre in Calgary, Alberta, was about to turn one hundred years old. The stage where I stood had played host to artists and dignitaries from around the world during its long and complicated history. My appearance was decidedly less auspicious than most, but it was important to me. What I did not know at the time was just how important it would be.

The speech I gave that day was a fourteen-minute contribution to a TEDx conference. TEDx events are independent creations set up by local organizers in conjunction with the hugely popular TED series (www.ted .com). TED has become an Internet sensation by combining the traditions of the public intellectual with emerging social media. My contribution was to be a discussion of a discovery I had made while researching and teaching at the University of Calgary. I titled my talk "Loving Communication." Actually, I do not believe I ever officially settled on that title, but that was the title that accompanied the video of the event that appeared three weeks later, and it seems to have stuck. During the course of my loosely structured talk, I suggested that we replace critical thinking in the university with an open-source, creative, loving model.

The event was quite enjoyable, and I believed that my talk had gone relatively well. I received many supportive messages, the magazine *Alberta Views* ran an excerpt in their education issue, and I got a lovely message from Chad Gaffeld, then president of the Social Sciences and Humanities

Research Council of Canada. The event had served the purpose that TED suggests it should, and I began an exciting conversation about these issues with people from a variety of geographic locations and intellectual traditions. If that were all that happened, I would probably not be writing this book.

Shortly after the talk was posted to YouTube, negative responses to it began flowing in. I was taken aback by this, for a few reasons. First, I did not really think that interest in my topic would last that long. I was mistaken. Second, I did not feel that what I had said was cogent or assertive enough to raise hackles. Again I was in error. Third, I realize that I am a relatively small player in the world of ideas, so the likelihood that anything I say will in any way impact someone else in the academy is extraordinarily small. I do not believe I was mistaken about my insignificance, but I was wrong about others' perceptions of it.

I want to share with you some of the ideas that were sent to me in response to my suggestion that we introduce loving thinking. But before I do so, I want to express my sincere gratitude to those who have taken the time to call and to write. My work in this area has been going on for several years now, but not until this commentary came in was I motivated enough to put down in book form the ideas that are at the heart of my current research. I also believe that it is important for me to accept responsibility for the way I presented my ideas during the TEDx event. My approach to their format was to speak in broad strokes in order to spark discussion, but it seems that the way in which I spoke has genuinely upset some people. That was certainly not my intention. The heart of the idea I want to share is that we have more to gain from creative, contributory engagement than through the traditional attack and parry of critical thinking. That said, I feel a duty to make my ideas clear so that those who wish to disagree have something tangible to which to respond. I hope we can extend the discussion that has come out of my talk and that I can clarify my position and offer some further thoughts on certain areas of the subject. I have been working on these issues for many years now and am glad to have the opportunity to share my work.

In that original talk, I detailed the discoveries I had made after I was hired to develop and teach a series of fine-arts-based courses that would appeal to students from all faculties on our campus. The University of Calgary is a large research institution with all of the traditional departments of other universities and a set of strong professional schools, so we have a wide variety of thinkers at work. The project was two years old by the time I was hired, by which time it had benefited from a large, multidisciplinary panel of interested academics and administrators. I was asked to take their findings, launch my own research, and after a year's time come up with some courses that I might offer on campus as pilot projects.

The short version of the story is that these courses became quite popular. That should not come as any surprise, given that they were designed for students using suggestions they had been submitting in national and local surveys for years. The surprising part related to how the classes worked and to the discoveries I made as part of the process. After a decade of teaching at the university level, applying the critical thinking model that remains the governing principle of modern universities, I concluded that the old way of working is broken. The changes happening in our world as the result of information technology, increased global communication, and a deeper understanding of human cognition require something more nuanced than a system of intellectual engagement based on a first-order linear model. Critical thinking peaked when the industrial model of work was predominant; this was fine in the nineteenth century, when people read a few handfuls of books each year, but how are we supposed to think critically about an object-oriented, networked world of information?

What I proposed was that rather than attacking and dissecting every bit of information that comes to us, we should become active contributors to the global conversation. Rather than listing problems, we should become engines for ideas and allow the best thinking to emerge organically from a process that welcomes all contributors. Imagine a discussion about Shakespeare's *Hamlet* that involves an engineer from Calgary, a doctor from Brazil, a dancer from Tokyo, a biologist from Tehran, and a writer from Texas. What is exciting about that interaction would not be the way we attack one another, but rather the ways we find to open our arms to our colleagues' ideas. We would have no need to worry about whose offering is best – the ideas would take care of themselves. This type of networked or shared conversation would stem from a creative way of thinking. It would place primary emphasis on hospitality, where critical approaches would foster suspicion.

A creative or contributory way of thinking would encourage sharing by providing a forum for discussion that privileged the creation of ideas rather than their destruction through narrowly focused rhetorical attack. This idea came about as a result of seeking ways that diverse groups of thinkers could work together to the best ends. When I took the time to reflect on what I was seeing, I realized that this type of work – a model where each person is constantly contributing new ideas – must be of interest to businesses, to governments, and to schools. I thought it might capture an opening that relates to cognition in the twenty-first century. We are talking about broader perspectives and the growing realization that our "no pain, no gain" approach to learning is wrong. Once we realize this, the world opens for us: we experience a feeling of spaciousness that comes from being more intellectually free.

Academics often share stories of great, serendipitous discoveries – in books, in archives, while wandering through library stacks, during visits to special collections, or in the dynamic mess of an active lab. The discoveries I was making as a result of designing some new option courses gave me that feeling, which has lasted to this day.

I am sure that as you read this you can tell that the experience of working in this new way has been something of an awakening for me. In fact, it is more like a return. Moving back toward creative thought returns us to the passions that brought us to academic study in the first place. It is only when our natural curiosities are constrained by the violence that pumps through the veins and arteries of critical thinking that we become timid, closed, and finally angry about the world of thought. We become institutionalized rather than independent thinkers.

Perhaps the best-known of all speeches on education is the 2006 TED talk given by Sir Ken Robinson.[1] In that talk he provides the spark for much of what I will be discussing. He points out that our schools are destroying our creative spirits, and he demands that something be done. He suggests a radical set of shifts in education. Robinson has spent his life working on education issues. He was a professor of education, and he now works with governments and organizations around the world and holds several research appointments. His focus is on the Western educational model, which – as he points out in his talk – has been adopted globally. That model is not something he feels we should celebrate; rather, we should fight to overturn it. Robinson places the blame on the hierarchical structure, one in which math and languages are at the top and the performing arts at the bottom. It functioned well for training workers for an industrial economy, but it destroys our creativity. Robinson feels we must pull the whole system down.

My approach is more radical than Robinson's but also simpler: I suggest that we stop teaching critical thinking in the university and begin to teach loving thinking. That is what I said in my TEDx talk, and that is what I continue to believe. And that, of course, is what got me into trouble.

The first sign that I had upset some people came via email. Once my talk was posted to YouTube, I began to receive threatening messages that asserted that my ideas would lead to the end of civilization. Some suggested that my ideas would unleash violence by the Bush administration (which was odd, given that George W. was no longer in office and had not been for quite some time); others equated them with equally dangerous liberal

policies. Almost all of these respondents attacked my character by draw-
ing broad conclusions about who and what I am – this on the basis of a
fourteen-minute speech.

I found this unnerving, but it did support my point: critical thinking
was causing us to attack one another rather than share ideas. Oddly, there
had been a time when critical thinking called upon us to see all sides of an
issue. Many of the angry messages I received – and there were and continue
to be a lot of them – responded to my ideas almost uniformly by suggesting that I should not be allowed to teach at the university. It seemed an odd
position to take, given the implications for freedom of speech and the academic tradition. Another surprising response came from those who were
eager to defend the life of the mind. I thought I was arguing for a *larger* life
of the mind, rather than for its cessation, but many saw it as the opposite.
They powerfully asserted that we must remain committed to teaching critical thinking to all students. The problem here that is I am not certain that I
should be teaching anyone how to think; instead, shouldn't I be supporting
my students' explorations of their own ways of thinking? To my mind, we
need diversity of thought if we are to best engage the future.

Shortly after this initial barrage of emails, a colleague at another institution contacted me. He explained that his department was "outraged" and
"furious" with what I had said and that they had appointed him to challenge
me to a debate. Their department had agreed to use their visiting lecturer
funds to bring me to campus to defend my ideas. He said that his colleagues
wanted him to "teach me a lesson." Again, I could not help but suspect that
this type of reaction supported my view that critical thinking had degraded
to the point where it no longer served ideas but instead promoted a kind of
violence in the academy. I responded that I would be more than happy to
visit and share ideas in some form of panel discussion where we could have
a wide-ranging conversation, or to present a paper with responses. However, my colleague was quite clear that this would not satisfy those who had
elected him to be my adversary. It had to be combat or nothing.

Fortunately for me, their organization took a long time to put their
event together, and by the time they contacted me again my speaking
schedule was full. I must admit that I continue to wonder whether I would
have fallen back into my old ways during such a debate and become what
I most wish to change – the aggressive, point-for-point debater who cares
about winning rather than contributing. Having been raised in the critical
school (as of course, we all have been), I feel that I will always have to keep
an eye on myself so that I do not fall back into my training as an intellectual
combatant. This recognition that deep grooves of malice have been carved
into our minds by critical thinking has led me to feel that we owe it to the

next generation of thinkers to free them from this broken system and allow them to see clearly once more.

The next round of contributions came from colleagues. Two of these stand out. In one, a senior scholar told me that my ideas were a "career killer" and that if I wished to pursue them it would be wise to keep them for the end of my working life, when I would no longer care that I was destroying myself professionally. This suggestion was made in the most caring of tones and with the utmost seriousness. It came from someone who declared herself a supporter of mine who was "in my corner." The boxing metaphor seemed apt. In the other, a careful scholar explained to me that my ideas made me sound mentally unstable. The advice was coupled with a discussion of mental health support and a helpful reminder that there was nothing shameful in seeking professional advice from a psychiatrist or psychologist. In that person's defence, I am rather energetic when speaking publicly, which may have caused concern. I truly think she thought she was being helpful.

As these comments piled up, I began to wonder just what I had wandered into with my fourteen-minute talk. I found that I kept returning to the same question: Why were people so angry at the suggestion that we embrace *creative* or *loving* thinking? Of course, those were just the idle thoughts of someone reacting to negative messages. I had become my own test subject. Over time, and with the support of friends and colleagues, I began to believe that the responses were so vehement because I had hit a nerve. The fight-or-flight response that is one of the biological determinants of critical thinking had been activated.

Clearly, my idea was important, and I needed to develop it further, but in such a way that I did not myself resort to critical thinking as a defence. How does one respond to violent attack? With discussion. With ideas. With loving, creative thought.

In this book, I trace the origins of critical thinking and suggest that since its historical beginnings in Plato's response to the death of his beloved teacher Socrates, it has contained elements of violence and anger as essential ingredients. When we examine the development and deployment of critical thinking from a historical perspective, we uncover its ongoing engagement with philosophies, theologies, and ideologies of aggression against self and other. Does this mean it was always and everywhere aggressive? Of course not. But by returning to the genesis of critical thought, perhaps we can uncover the lost, neglected strain of open, creative, and loving thought that at one time was seen as equal to the critical path and indeed as its more mature expression.

Having located critical thinking in time, we will turn our attention to its operating procedures. In doing so, we will discover that in all places and at all times, this mode of work has involved language of aggression. What does this say about our educational system? About our society? By evaluating examples, we will uncover the propensity of critical argument to degrade into *ad hominem* or character attack. From the earliest discussions of ideas, attack on character was seen as the lowest form of argument, yet it seems today to be the most common. Once we identify the nature of critical operations, we begin to glimpse how this mode of communication hampers our abilities to operate in the academy and in the public and private spheres.

Some of the most exciting discoveries in this burgeoning field come when we ask new questions about our thinking and working lives. Does anyone in business really want more critical thinkers? The short answer is no. Business leaders are clamouring for innovators, entrepreneurs, and inventors, but those are *creative* skills, not critical ones. Does it not follow that business would be better served by an education system that emphasized creative thinking? Do governments need more critics? Our system of government is based on a form of critical thinking first established in ancient Greece. Does anyone think it is still working? Or are we continually asking ourselves why this system will not allow us to work together more effectively? Finally, do the universities need more critics? Is anyone *asking* for more critics? Is anyone running short on them, or struggling to fill critical thinking positions? Again, the answer is no. Instead, the academy is desperate for *creative* thinkers who will engage the Internet age, global warming, secular and pluralist ethics, public and social policy, and the frontiers of medicine – to name only a few areas. When we study the realities of the moment in which we find ourselves, the decision seems clear. A move to an educational and epistemological model that emphasizes creative rather than critical thought could address concerns in all areas of our world.

This new model of thinking also better suits our current lives. Critical thinking is a simple, linear model. It deals with data in relational terms. Our world is more dynamic, object-oriented, and networked. Creativity scales to our new, networked world; critical thinking simply cannot keep up. There is too much information to spend time attacking everything. Instead, we should more fully embrace information and grow our creative engagement with the expanding connections being offered to us.

The type of change I am talking about must go beyond politics – or at least politics in its ideological modes. We are not talking about progressive political change, or a revolution, or a conservative approach to a return to a liberal arts model of education. This change is a correction of a misstep on the path to expression, a necessary alteration to fine-tune the way we live and work. Our current situation requires that we change. For me, this is an evolution of thought, of communication, and of being. Our moment may well be larger than any other in history, and it requires a shift equal to the call that is being sent. Let us be clear, though, this will require more and not less work. Any suggestion that the Digital Age will somehow make life easier has long since been abandoned.

One of the challenges of living in a world of critical thinkers is that it has become too deeply committed to us-versus-them thinking. As a consequence, educational reform, change, or transformation is too often seen in competitive, political terms. Creative change is beyond the old, narrow purview of politics. This change is about our lives, right here, right now. It has the potential to free us from the narrow, linear traps that have come to define local and national politics and religious and ideological divides. Thought as conflict is what we did in our early days; it is now time to leave that period behind and enter the next phase of our engagement with our global family. We need loving thinking.

Since I am proposing a broad-based change, this book opens its arms wide. I believe it is important for us to engage this subject with as broad an audience as possible, so I will avoid specialist language and beg your forgiveness if you feel the text is overly simple in places related to your particular expertise. It is my sincere hope that I will have time to write follow-up pieces that can go into more detail, and that others will join this discussion so that we may re-evaluate the way we train ourselves to think. If you feel that your area of research requires greater detail in this discussion, please accept this small book as your invitation to begin writing.

As with its starting place, this book is in one sense a fool's exercise. It will certainly cause frustration among some of our colleagues, but believe me when I say that is not my intention. I firmly believe that an open discussion of the matters introduced in this book will prove fruitful for all involved. I am certain that I will make – indeed, have already made – many mistakes. This book is only meant to start the discussion. Other brighter and bigger minds can take it from there. The fool's role is to say the thing that no one else is saying, but that we are all thinking.

The book, of necessity, will be brief and broad. It is meant to be accessible to everyone working on our campuses and everyone who has an interest in what goes on there. For that reason, specialists will find the questions asked and solutions suggested to be general starting points. I hope they will take this as an invitation to do future work in the area. As part of this approach, examples will all be drawn from general public knowledge. Please do not take this as support for or criticism of current political structures. I am just trying to speak in a way that we can all understand. The compensation for the general nature of the book is its brevity and – hopefully – clarity.

For this project to be of use, I can only hope you will join me in following Rumi's instructions at the top of my preface: "Out beyond ideas of wrongdoing and rightdoing, there is a field. I'll meet you there."

Will you meet me there?

Chapter 2

The Baby and the Bathwater

The Birth of Critical Thinking

In 399 BCE, Socrates tipped back a cup of hemlock and escaped the world of critical thought for good.[1] It wasn't a suicide. At least it wasn't a regular suicide. Rather, he took one of a few options presented to him after he had been convicted of corrupting the youth of his city. He could have chosen to flee, but he saw no reason to avoid death, so, surrounded by his faithful students, he ended his life. The events of that day continue to define the way we teach and think today.

What Socrates had done that was so unnerving for the powers that be who gave him that fateful choice, was to ask pointed questions that made their targets uncomfortable. In an age of travelling debaters, Socrates was more interested in meaning than in rhetorical flourish. His was a practice that often embarrassed people publicly, and his students were ardent supporters of his methods. It is from the ashes of these early interrogations that we derive the critical thinking we practise today.

Among the crowds that followed the old master was an especially sharp young student named Plato. Soon after the elder scholar's death, heart-broken over the loss of his master, he would develop the outline for an ideal state that would exclude poets and any type of writing or speech that was not regimented by a precisely defined form of reason.[2] His ideal world would do away with those he believed were responsible for his master's death.[3] Who could blame the young man for fantasizing about a world that would exclude those who had robbed him of his mentor?

The book Plato wrote was called *The Republic,* and it remains one of the most influential books in the world. Strangely, while his words overtly attacked the creative, his writing was itself artistic. He captured his hero Socrates in countless dialogues winning argument after argument and putting his enemies in their place. These dialogues remain as entertaining as they are elucidating. Socrates lives on through Plato's elaborate memorial and stands as a monument to critical thought.

Ever since that cup of poison, readers of Plato have added a grain of salt to the more vitriolic components of the injured student's philosophy. No one – or almost no one – questions his brilliance, but many have struggled with the seeming bitterness that bubbles up occasionally in his work. His critical framework contains elements of revenge that retain their power to this day.

Another student who was present on that fateful day when Socrates lifted the cup was Aristotle. The young Aristotle was the first and still the greatest to pick up on Plato's anger and to generously attempt to soften the older student's blows. That struggle, which centred on the inclusion or exclusion of creative thinking in Plato's ideal city, is at the heart of the challenges we face today.

Aristotle contributed to the struggle in another, unintended way by introducing two-part logic. Right and wrong, this or not this, a or not a – all models like these go back to Aristotle. His logic was a great gift to the Western tradition, but its strictures when coupled with Socratic questioning created a form of oppositional relationship that is conducive to combat rather than communion.

Currently, critical thinking is more a religion than a system of thought. It is so thoroughly ingrained in our institutions that we no longer wonder whether it should be a fundamental component of all education. Teachers, researchers, and academic administrators all promise to teach us to "think critically." We actually guarantee – overtly or implicitly – that all graduating students will be critical thinkers by the time we are done with them. Why do we accept so unquestioningly that learning to think critically is a good thing? Is there a shortage of criticism in our world? Where did this mantra of education and self-development come from?

So, critical thinking has an illustrious past. It also has an impressive scope. In fact, it is safe to say that critical thinking lies at the heart of all of today's educational systems, East and West. In his now famous TED talk, Sir Ken Robinson challenges us to re-examine the way we are educating children for the twenty-first century. He points out that all schools on earth have the same hierarchy in terms of subjects and in the parts of the body we train. We train ourselves "from the neck up and mostly to one side," according to Robinson. I contend that the engine behind this training is critical thinking. It dominates world education and may well be the only universally agreed upon educational goal. Yet we never seem to question the questioning. Instead, critical thinking exists like the Wizard of Oz, pulling levers behind the scenes and warning us firmly to pay no attention to its operations.

As Robinson points out, the Western model of education stemming from Socrates, Plato, and Aristotle dominates global education. So when we speak of the problems of pedagogy and critical thinking, it is reasonable to suppose we are addressing everyone involved in learning. We may decry the inequities that led to the uniform adoption of this form of education, but as Robinson points out, we cannot deny its pervasive influence.

One other way in which critical thinking now resembles a religion more than an intellectual pursuit is that it now verges on a sacrilege to question its value. Yet the dictates of critical thought actually *require* us to question assumptions. How interesting, then, that we are not allowed to question the system that commands us to question. Politicians often speak of issues that will kill a campaign as "the third rail." They are referencing the power rail of the subway or train that kills on contact. How did we arrive at a place where critical thought has become the third rail of intellectual life? How did it become this strong? It turns out that we can trace the transformation alongside the development of intellectual history.

The story of critical thought in the West – and we should be clear that this is only one possible story among many – begins with Socrates and his response to the group now called the Presocratics. Eastern critical thought explores similar issues in different ways and can be studied in places such as the early Buddhist studies of being and living in society, but for our purposes, we will focus on the Western tradition, which ended up taking over global education. What does it mean for our educational system that its foundations lie in the imaginings of a heartbroken student trying to keep his teacher alive?

When the French philosopher Michel Foucault looked back on the legacy of the Greeks, he reminded us of an important distinction.[4] Education for the students of the Classical world involved two separate streams, both of which were necessary for people to realize their full potential as citizens. The first was to "know thyself," and the pursuit of this goal remains at the heart of modern academe. Critical thinking in its early forms, with its ability to take in information and then analyze, synthesize, and evaluate it, was a useful tool when pursuing this direction. Along the way, however, we forgot the second stream – to "care for the self," that is, to develop yourself into the fullest extent so that you could best serve your fellow citizens.[5] It seems that the loss of this side of the dyad left the first stream vulnerable to degradation when left alone.

Critical thinking works well when analyzing oneself, but creative thought is necessary to follow the second path, which for the Greeks was the more important goal. Plato's banishment of the creative threw out fully half the project for human development. So it is not surprising that if we ask again, "Is there a lack of criticism in our world? Are people going without sufficient levels of criticism?," and extend the exercise to ask, "Are people asking for better ways to care for themselves, to develop themselves or to be creative?," the answers perfectly demonstrate the state of disharmony in which we find ourselves. We want less criticism and more creativity.

In his desire to recuperate the reputation of his lost master and to punish his perceived enemies, the young Plato allowed his philosophy to be tainted by his hurt and his anger. That same hurt and anger echoes through contemporary critical thought. By foregrounding critical thinking that descends from this model, we are training ourselves to be able but angry naysayers. There was no real problem with this as long as the creation of primary texts outweighed that of critical commentary. Part of the challenge came when we began to build our educational systems in such a way as to provide vastly greater support for criticism than for poetry and other such work. Our universities – and the schools we have designed to feed them – function as models of the ideal Platonic society. Following Plato, we provide very little support for the creative arts and focus almost entirely on criticism.

When Ken Robinson called out for a transformation of the academy, one of his key points focused on how the disciplines are presently ranked: languages and math at the top, the fine arts at the bottom. And at that bottom, the fine arts are further divided into categories that place the embodied arts – drama and dance – at the *very* bottom. Robinson asks why we do not teach dance in every school. He argues that we are following a model of education that was designed to support the Industrial Revolution and its need for methodical workers who sat still. He is right, but only partly. The challenges he highlights developed during the very birth of Western (and later taken up by Eastern) civilization; from the start, they have dominated our systems of learning and modes of thought. Those systems peaked many centuries later, during the industrial age, and are now collapsing everywhere around the world.

Critical thought since Plato has been rooted in suspicion. As a system, it is designed to receive information: it breaks data down into their constituent components and tests for any and all weaknesses. This approach to communication was forged by an angry and helpless young student who rejected his society and wished to implement his own vision, one in which he and his friends would be hailed as the supreme arbiters of all aspects of daily life.

Socrates, as presented by Plato, levels attack after attack on the Sophists, a travelling band of teachers who prepared citizens to present their cases in the public forum.[6] In Plato's view, these predecessors to modern-day lawyers were responsible for Socrates's death, so he attacked them with predictable harshness when he recorded their interactions with the great critical master. When one person controls all aspects of the debate, the outcome can easily be manipulated for content and effect. Of course, Plato was far too serious a thinker to be consumed by his emotional bond with his philosophic master. While the residual trauma that inflects his ideas is of particular interest in this book, I am not seeking to dim the vast constellation of discoveries attributed to Socrates's star student.

The story of Thrasymachus is one of the most popular in the Socratic tradition.[7] An old Sophist, who seems almost too angry for words, builds an argument in *The Republic* that seems ready-made for attack. For years, people have discussed the Thrasymachus story as a study in freedom of speech.[8] While that argument is not found in the text, it has been a point of discussion for generations of thinkers.

In the story, we find ourselves in the *agora* or public space – a place where all free individuals have the right to express themselves. The commitment to ideas is total. But in the case of Thrasysmachus, this commitment is put to its ultimate test. The question that gets bandied about goes something like this: What do we do if one person is arguing in such a way that they are shutting down the ability of others to speak? At what point does freedom of speech require us to silence one voice so that others may be heard? Part of this discussion involves the idea that Thrasymachus, as a Sophist, may be guilty of intellectual nihilism – in some readings he is trying to shut down discussion merely for his own enjoyment.

The case is a fascinating one and has fuelled armchair philosophy for hundreds of years. In the end, Socrates manages to stop him, but we are left with an exception that may prove the rule that we may need to deny some figures the right to speak. Contentious stuff, this.

For me, the story of the cranky old Sophist carries another question: If the *agora* was a space committed to free-flowing ideas, what if there had been a way to make it freer? It would not have been that hard an exercise – after all, when the *agora* was established, only a tiny percentage of Greeks even qualified as persons. But beyond extending the franchise, within the circle of those declared free we must ask: Could the rules of engagement have hampered the free flow of ideas?

Forgive my fondness for the artists of the time. Had it not been for Plato's petulant dismissal of the arts, we could have made better use of the explorations that occurred in the play competitions and in the recited poetry of the Greek tradition. Many feel that Aristophanes's plays may have been responsible for the attack on Socrates. When Plato privileged reason over all else, he erected a bully pulpit from which he never descended.[9] Twenty-five hundred years later, when Ken Robinson points out that the hierarchy of education is broken, its malfunction bears an eerie mark of those early predispositions. That hierarchy, which Plato sketched out in *The Republic,* and which echoes through several of his works, reflects a world where reason dominates and the arts are rejected with prejudice. Such is the power of his rhetoric that we are still in the grip of a broken-hearted student's lamentations after generations of other thinkers have come and gone.

Aristotle, the younger of Socrates's two famous students, was a more methodical and thus a decidedly less sensational thinker. His work often served as a corrective to some of his senior colleague's bolder claims. Famously, of his writings on creative matters, only his reflections on the genre of tragedy have been preserved. His writings on comedy, the more celebratory of the forms, have been lost to time, and as a consequence, greater weight has accrued around tragedy's more serious approach to the world.[10] Still, even in this forum, Aristotle pointed out the positive contribution made by creative forces.[11] Plato wanted to control information; Aristotle wanted to free it for the good of society. For Plato, the artist had no *techné,* that is, no refined skill; for Aristotle, the *techné* of the artist was of the highest order. It was the creation of something new that had value.

We live in the wake of the debate started by these two brilliant students. Their arguments over censorship, art, and communication remain at the centre of public life. The British and American decision to embed reporters during the conflict in Iraq echoes an ancient policy promoted by Plato: only those stories that support the society's warrior heroes should be told – all other narratives weaken the resolve of the citizenry. The US government's active support of pro-military films such as 2001's *Pearl Harbor* are likewise in keeping with the thinking that underpins Plato's ideal society: story is only to be used in service of the state, and any dialogue that threatens the state should be controlled. Plato's ideas in this area were developed as a programmatic distribution of power and as a system of maintaining its operations. When neither their ideas nor their heroes could preserve this power, the Greeks were absorbed by the Roman Empire.

The Roman Empire is remembered as grand for a host of reasons. A key one, perhaps, was its policy of preserving the cultures of the societies it overthrew.[12] The Roman Empire gave shelter to the ideas of the Greek philosophers and the creations of its artists. It also mixed in its own capacity for violence.[13] Philosophy was militarized, and Roman plays became gory demonstrations of the more metaphoric violence we encounter in the Greek ones. Even comedy became far more physical and aggressive.

Debate, with publicly declared winners and losers, was a central component of Roman society.[14] Lives were lost and won in cleverly worded verbal attacks. They still are. Our schoolchildren still study the prowess with which Mark Antony brings scrutiny upon Brutus for his part in Caesar's death in Shakespeare's *Julius Caesar*.

Just as we feed our schoolchildren Shakespeare, so Shakespeare's teachers fed him the Latin classics. Hours spent translating and reciting the great Latin texts taught the children of his day the powerful tools of rhetoric, tools that Shakespeare would later pick up when framing many of his greatest scenes. In *Much Ado about Nothing,* verbal attack and parry with potentially lethal consequences becomes a delightful set of jousts between Beatrice and Benedict. But even in Shakespeare's artfully presented debate, the stakes are high – public humiliation and violent language are part of the engine of this popular comedy, which involves public ridicule, physical assault, and the proclamation of transgressions against decorum.

In the powerful cultural legacy of the Roman Empire, one story retains a special place. The teachings of a Jew from Nazareth became the hinge for extraordinary acts of both kindness and violence. This young upstart challenged old ideas with public verbal attacks, and he – like Socrates before him – chose to allow himself to be a victim of the state. He – again like Socrates – is linked in a significant way to how critical thinking has been passed down to us. As the Roman state and then Christianity took root, each injected aggression into human thought, and in doing so, constrained peaceful, loving ways of being. In the process, they turned to Plato for morality, to Aristotle for structure.

A famous example of how Rome and Christianity teamed up to support a more critical view of the world involves Epicurus.[15] The philosophy of Epicurus, which preached a joy in living, came to be saddled with false accusations of vice and licentiousness and was all but eliminated. At the same time, female thinkers of the pagan tradition were tortured and killed. Key to all this was the concept of heresy – of speaking in the wrong way, in a way against the state. As with Plato's ideal state, those in power sought to control what was said in the public sphere. Tellingly, personal and public acts of abuse became part of what was viewed as the ideal life. The life of the mind and the pursuit of creative work were devalued, while walking down the street lashing oneself with thorny branches was deemed an exemplary form of observance. In their attempts to please God, individuals became

their own oppressors. The mind was turned against the flesh. If Epicureanism was the wildness that must be tamed, then asceticism was the answer:
it is the criticism of the flesh.

Out of a small set of plain speeches by Christ grew a mountain of critical discourse preaching the word of a violently angry God who demanded
that He be appeased. Just as in Classical Greece, the more violent, less
thoughtful factions came to the fore, and we have lived with the consequences ever since. Long letters to the faithful prescribing aggressive piety
have buried Christ's simple message. Jesus spoke of peace and of contributory ways of being, and the Romans executed him for it. That many of his
followers became more Roman than Christian is telling.

It is from this tradition that we have inherited the texts that built our
universities. It is from this tradition that we have built our governmental
systems around the practice of public attack and parry known as political
debate. After the Germanic tribes – whose violence did not tarry for discussion – broke up the Roman Empire, these ideas lay dormant for a time,
but they were preserved, and then reintroduced by the Roman Church
throughout much of the world. They were presented most fervently in
continental Europe and Great Britain, and from there they have extended
around the globe.

When the intellectual treasures of the Classical world began to be
unearthed in the monasteries, they were subject to strict controls. Heed-
ing Plato, the church hierarchy carefully governed what could be read,
heard, or said. Even so, small moments of creativity shone through. Scribes
inserted playful comments while copying texts; households could interpret
those texts for themselves; and in private, individuals could write their own
reflections on books both old and new. People danced at home.

Thinking to benefit from the ancient power of drama, church leaders
began allowing theatrical presentations of approved messages. Not surprisingly, these performances began to show signs of returning to the deeper
exploration of ideas, which had been their original purpose. In this long
process, creative bursts came through. In England, the distribution and
creative reworking of William Langland's *Piers Plowman* helped greatly to
incite for the 1381 Peasants' Revolt.[16] Reading was directly linked to performance – to an embodied engagement with knowledge that both the schools
and the church disallowed.

When the church and some of the trade guilds were given permission to stage regular festivals of performance, this opened the door for the
English Renaissance to enter. Creative expression exploded. Not long after
the millers' and weavers' pageants came Christopher Marlowe, who demonstrated the power of a more creative and less critically controlled use

of drama. When Marlowe defied the dictates of Classical formalism, the English Renaissance began.[17] Actually, there had been other renaissances before this, but this was the one – along with its slightly older continental cousin – that we refer to most often in schools and in Western discourse.

The wild, freethinking messages of the Renaissance were carried along on a wave of new technology. The printing press changed everything. The ability to mass-produce texts presented a powerful challenge to those in authority who wished to follow Plato's ideas about the control of information. The Roman Church, once the absolute ruler of information, found itself threatened by this technology and by a violent argument within its own ranks. Protestant radicals unintentionally shattered the Platonic control of information by demanding that all citizens be able to read the Bible for themselves.

The West was experiencing a revolution in thought. The church could no longer control the emergence of ideas, and eventually, after imprisoning or killing as many apostates as it could, it accepted that a revolution in human understanding was inevitable and began crafting new arguments that would allow it to maintain as much control as possible.

Well before all of this, toward the end of the Roman Empire, Saint Augustine had written long arguments defending the church and attacking its enemies. His *City of God* followed Plato's pattern: it created a new argument for an ideal society, this one with an all-powerful and endlessly displeased God at the helm. It is a work of critical brilliance and remains a world classic, but its commitment to rational argument and to the restriction of creative thought is corrosive. Augustine was one of the first great minds to commit time to critical argument in the service of church doctrine. In his church, as in many other world religions, legions of thinkers have trained a critical eye on issues of faith – or rather, on anything that questions their definition of faith. Both formal theologians and those apologists who try to reconcile faith and reason have committed themselves to a form of controlled, itemized, well-constructed argument. Almost all of these writers combine Plato's commitment to the control of information with Aristotle's attention to taxonomy and quality of logical presentation, following the right-versus-wrong model with which we are all so familiar.

Centuries later, Thomas Aquinas would claim the mantle of chief critic for the church. His attempts to reconcile Aristotle with Catholic doctrine are magnificent demonstrations of the power of critical thinking to mash together the rational requirements of well-formed arguments and the mystical elements of Christian metaphysics. They also demonstrate that critical thinking does not lead to truth; instead, it leads to stronger and stronger versions of what you want to believe.

Saint Thomas Aquinas emerged after the textual Dark Age that fell upon the West when the Germanic tribes ended the Roman Empire's dominance. In the West, we often think of the tale of *Beowulf* as representative of this time. There is something dark and dangerous about this warrior's tale. It comes to us in only one copy and bears the mark of a Christian scribe who attempted to rework its message in order to present a different tale than the story contains.[18] It is Christianity imposed on a world that will not have it.

The provenance of *Beowulf* remains a point of debate, but this story, whether in the original or in translation, is held up as an indicator of the violence of the times when European textuality was in the dark. Today's liberal arts education begins the study of culture with *Beowulf* and its fellows, and we cannot help but notice the differences between pre-Christian narratives and those religiously inflected and refined books that dominate our reading lists.

One of the first texts we encounter that reminds us of our world is Geoffrey Chaucer's *The Canterbury Tales*. Tellingly, this first literary bestseller contains multiple stories involving incredible violence. Chaucer drew those stories from the Classical period and reworked them for contemporary audiences. They are framed by the narrative of people competing to tell stories in public for a prize. Within that frame, the storytellers attack one another and must be governed by a representative of the military who is part of the travelling group. It is competitive, militarized debate, with the state as the arbiter.

In the warrior boasts of *Beowulf* and in the story competitions of *The Canterbury Tales*, we see the traces of speech as a tool for dominance. Our current open mic, spoken word, and poetry slam forms are keeping these ancient competitive traditions alive thousands of years after they were first conceived. Political debate retains the oppositional and violent forces of its predecessors but has degraded to the point where complex rhetoric and the discussion of ideas are all but gone. But let's not get ahead of ourselves …

To return to our dramatists, after Marlowe, Shakespeare was able to practise with a type of creative freedom that had not been seen for hundreds of years. The acknowledged master of the English language faced no set grammar and no formal rules of spelling to hold him back. In this unfettered environment, and in an atmosphere of ideas supported by William Caxton's importation of Gutenberg's printing press,[19] the creative world exploded.[20] It is hard for us to imagine the freedom that ungoverned language offers. The students to whom we teach Shakespeare's work are told there are strict grammatical rules that must be followed, and they are docked for spelling mistakes. Such a regimen is almost the opposite of the freedom that gave rise to the greatest era of exploration in our language. How strange that we idolize such a wildly free writer with essays that must conform to tight little boxes policed by experts with guidebooks full of invented laws.

On the European continent, a similar explosion happened, but earlier and with a different set of arts at the heart of the movement. Just as in England, thinkers returned to the great texts of the Classical period and used freedom of thought as a means to challenge religious and political norms – they were trying to reboot the system. In painting, in music, and in writing, creativity was fuelled by open access to ideas. The true fuel of the Renaissance was the free flow of information. Print technology, as well as a mindset that did not yet think of ideas as something to be commoditized, sold, and protected by law, provided a type of *agora* where creativity could reassert itself. Around the same time, the idea re-emerged that human beings might be allowed to pursue lives that were not committed to apology, proselytizing, or self-flagellation; instead they could celebrate life, beauty, and the pursuit of a better way of living.

While scientists, philosophers, artists, and others battled with the church over a wave of new discoveries, an expanded version of critical thinking began to take root. Those who were called to testify before tribunals to defend new ideas found themselves ensnared in highly skilled critical arguments. Through public and private trials, the church and the dominant political structures sought to control information in the manner first suggested by Plato. To lose one of these public arguments meant death by torture.

By the time the hard boot of the Reformation came down on the creative class of England and Europe, a great reawakening of the need for a *care of the self* through creative engagement had left an indelible mark on human cognition. The strength of those who fought against the creativity found in the science, technology, and arts of the time came from two distinct sources passed down from the Classical period: physical violence, and a muscular, linear form of thought. It makes sense: if you want to control information and train citizens to think in a particular way, you need a highly structured and regulated system of education. And that's just what we got.

Critical thinking, wielded by expert critical thinkers, was used to attack Galileo and the public theatres alike. Critical thinking was used to argue against the use of the vernacular in science, religion, and the arts. Critical thinking sent people to death and shuttered the theatres. Critical thinking – like the sophistry that Plato thought it would combat – was weaponized. Its enemies were citizens, scientists, artists, and philosophers. To avoid severe penalties – including, very often, death – one had to publicly affirm critical thinking and atone for the sin of non-compliance. You had to become reasonable.

Fortunately for freethinking Europeans, the internecine warfare in Christianity meant there would never again be one dominant church in the way there had been for so many centuries. The freedom this rift afforded came at a heavy price, but once that price had been paid, the continent saw itself flourish in the period known as the Enlightenment.[21] As with the term "the Renaissance," the Enlightenment means many things to many people today. That said, its great unifying triumph was to firmly establish a political place for free thought.

We do not often think of the Enlightenment as primarily a creative time; rather, we see it as a mainly scientific and philosophic revolution that asserted itself politically. But not everyone sees it that way. Remember our definition of creativity: the creation of something new that has value. If we accept that definition, then the Enlightenment was an age of creativity. Enlightenment figures like Spinoza, Newton, and Voltaire were opening the door for a broad-based return to a presocratic engagement with human life. Enlightenment creatives picked up critical thinking and turned it back on the institutions that had been using it to suppress human flourishing since Plato.

But this fecundity had costs. The philosophical commitment to reason strengthened some of the totalitarian tendencies of critical thinking. Given its systemic commitment to either/or Aristotelian logic, this outcome was inevitable. (Tellingly, Spinoza's exploration of new mathematical forms led to some of the freest speech in philosophical thought in our tradition.) In France there was talk of scientists being the *best* or most useful citizens in the realm.[22] When we hear such talk, we are immediately reminded of Plato's citizen-servants. In the end, though, there were many rulers who were better than those they had replaced, and those who challenged the opponents of freedom of thought retained enough strength to open the world to the Romantics.

The Romantic period arrives on our historical march just in time to caution us against overemphasizing the importance of the anarchic elements of creative pursuits by human beings and groups. Just as the Enlightenment had seemed a little too Apollonian for the creative mind, so the Romantic period came to be a little too Dionysian for its own good. As a result, its contributions to the dialogue about a world that was being transformed by the Industrial Revolution came mostly in the form of abstract or symbolic protest. A lone figure who had rejected the advent of organized urban life could do little to incite social change on the streets of the burgeoning cities that inspired their disdain.

One of the most powerful voices in the Romantic movement was that of Jean-Jacques Rousseau.[23] He was so deeply committed to truth that he published an autobiography so personal that it still takes one's breath away. A famous example is a long passage on the pleasure he received from being spanked as a not-so-young boy. Rousseau tapped into the power of personal authenticity when he challenged organized power on behalf of the individual. He would forever change thinking about education and psychology. But for the purposes of our discussion, it was Friedrich Nietzsche who presented the most significant challenge to the roots of power in critical thought.

Nietzsche was a wild and original thinker.[24] Not since Spinoza had anyone so completely challenged the received history of human thought. By returning to the presocratics and testing the power matrices established by the twin tensions of the Apollonian and the Dionysian modes of thinking, he challenged the use of critical thought as a path to truth. He asserted that poetry should take pride of place in the philosopher's project, and he railed against the stultifying effects of the hyper-rational inheritors of the version of Socrates presented to us by his students.

According to Nietzsche, the Judeo-Christian belief system had been designed for an enslaved and uneducated herd.[25] For the sake of freedom and the pursuit of knowledge, one had to reach back to the pagan traditions – those connected with Heraclitus and later Epicurus – that had been stamped out by the rational actors of the Classical world and later entombed by their Abrahamic successors. Nietzsche had uncovered a violent, oppressive force in language. As a young scholar, he had written critical treatises on Classical figures; now, for his great works, he moved to a poetic form of writing. In both form and content he struggled against the repressive bonds of critical thinking.

After Nietzsche, thinking in the West would come to be dominated by the question of language that had been part of his great discovery. In the Anglo-American tradition (following Ludwig Wittgenstein)[26] and in the Continental one (following Martin Heidegger), the late-modern and postmodern periods would be consumed by a fascination with language.[27] This "linguistic turn" affected all areas of the academy in terms of both research and teaching.[28] That same turn continues to define our world.[29]

Not surprisingly, in an academy fascinated with language, critical thinking was an attractive option, for it promised a controlled, testable, and repeatable approach to writing and speech. This book suggests that we have lost track of just what critical thinking is and that we have begun to take for granted that it is an inherently good thing to not only think critically but also to live critical thinking as a kind of religion – to *become* critical thinkers. Such a life has its rewards. By committing yourself to critical thinking and taking a never-ending oppositional stance, you can produce an endless stream of seemingly new research. This is a "factory model" that reminds us of Henry Ford's assembly line and the industrial universities that were developed to serve the Industrial Age and the Fordist economy. I suggest we discuss the *value* of that research and the type of teaching it promotes.

I have presented this brief overview of Western history to point out the links to violence and information control that critical thinking has forged over time. I by no means believe that these are concrete connections or that they are complete in any sense. It is, however, quite possible to demonstrate that violence and issues of control are present whenever and wherever we encounter critical thinking. Most often our intellectual archaeology makes such discoveries in tightly controlled environments such as schools, governments, and churches. The reasons for this are myriad, and while the connections are not by any means entirely negative, they are significant.

A number of scholars have explored violence in language and how it is used to repress various groups or exclude them from the unfolding story of human thought.[30] Other thinkers have examined how language has been used to control populations and exercise power.[31] Most often the focus is on the misbehaviour of powerful figures or the failings of language. But what if it is the *system of thought* itself that acts as a delivery mechanism for aggression? What if critical thinking is poisoning the well of human understanding and expression before thought even has a chance to begin? What if, instead of language, it is something *before* language and simpler – the binary separation of "this or not this," "*a* or not *a*," "right or wrong"?

What if, instead of patriarchs, oligarchs, sexists, and racists, the true originators of violent language were those who gave us critical thinking? If that were the case, then the mode of thought itself would serve those with nefarious purposes well, but it would have prefigured their individual pursuits of dominance. Further to this, what if, when wielding that same set of practices in order to defend ourselves against its more powerful encroachments, we begin to sacrifice our true selves to a system of thought that lends itself to aggression? – to winners and losers and to the public humiliation of the vanquished by the victor?

My hope is that you can take my rapid journey through the history of thought as I have intended – as one possible reading. My goal is to ask simple questions that will allow us to revisit our own knowledge and our intellectual past so that we wonder if we do not spot a tendency for critical thought to be inflected with the flavours of Roman aggression and Platonic repression. Of course, each of the periods I have mentioned could be the subject of a new book, and I hope they will be. For now, the goal of this project is merely to begin the discussion.

Several issues pertaining to our present circumstances seem to cry out for a new engagement with thought. Currently, we tell ourselves, prospective students, governments, and private backers that one thing we do at the university is train people in critical thought so that they leave our tutelage as critical thinkers. But is that what they need in order to live and work in the twenty-first century? This book asks whether there might be some benefit to revisiting these claims. Let us take a quick look at the revolution surrounding us and consider the ways it is being ill served by our unquestioning commitment to critical thinking.

The background to everything we say or do these days is the revolution in information technology and the ways it connects to globalism. We are living in the time of the single greatest change in the way that human beings communicate in history. No matter how much time we spend on this topic it will never be enough to capture the magnitude of this change.

In an earlier study, I called our current situation the *Second Incunabulum*. The *Incunabulum* refers to the period when we moved from manuscript to print technology. That period of change underpinned the explosion that was the Renaissance. We now find ourselves standing on a wave far higher than that of the first revolution, and the change is much more rapid. All of our questions bear the influence of the digital. The symptoms of this moment are anxiety and a resistance of change born out of the fear brought on by the sheer magnitude of the transformation facing us. Similar things were said when print began to replace manuscripts as the primary means of information technology several hundred years ago.

Critical thinking in its current form, with its deep ties to print technology, evaluates arguments in a methodical, linear fashion. Much like early computer technology, which focused on relational models of databases, critical thought tests for sound reasoning, logical connections, and validity. But can you realistically expect to evaluate all the information coming at you today using that old model?

When computers entered the equation, it became apparent that relational data modelling simply would not work as databases increased exponentially in size. So we moved to object-oriented work and more dynamic systems for engaging with information. These models highlight a more contributory method of information processing and have allowed multiple voices to participate in our language sets. Simply put, older models of computation were built like arguments from the traditions of critical thinking; newer models are more creative and dynamic and use less control.

If language matters – and surely it does – then what does it mean that most of our information now comes to us through open, active systems that grow organically? Is the best way of thinking about this world to use a system of thought based on two individuals standing opposite each other and taking turns debating each other? If 1,100 people from around the world are contributing to an online research project, do I really want to worry about who is winning? To put it more directly, why would I want to begin my thinking with a suspicious mind that starts from a position of "attack first, ask questions later"?

Critical thinking as a model of thought, even without its curious history, is an exhausted platform that needs to be replaced as the governing tenet of our educational systems. If we do not wish to give it up because of its violent, oppressive past, we must certainly leave it behind because it is not sufficiently complex to capture the information a citizen of the twenty-first century engages with while having breakfast.

Closely connected to the Information Revolution is the transformation brought about by globalization. That word means many different things, but in terms of human communication, it refers to the fact that we are increasingly in direct contact with more and more people from more and more places. How should we manage these conversations? Can we imagine a successful exchange based on a model where someone is a winner and another is a loser? Should we not instead be moving to a more open, contributory, and hospitable means of engagement?

In Classical times, religious figures with an interest in controlling information warned of a place where many languages were spoken simultaneously so that the din from all the voices together became a torture. The story of the Tower of Babel supported the notion of one true language that would be the arbiter of taste, truth, and social order.[32] Now the tower is everywhere, and much to the chagrin of those who would prefer we let our leaders govern international conversations, the sound is more like a symphony than a cacophony. There are translators and programs to learn new languages. The response to multiple voices is to educate ourselves – to dive *into* information, and to speak to one another directly and openly.

Here again, critical thinking is of little use. It has always been the property of a trained elite, and its obsession with the minutiae of argument makes it too clumsy a tool when we are trying to converse with people who speak different languages and have had different cultural experiences. Creative response, open engagement, and loving practice all work well. Critical thinking trains you to be suspicious of every assertion – to cut it up, evaluate it, test it, and then respond. Loving thinking calls for us to begin by giving the other the benefit of the doubt. You begin with open arms, not with scalpel in hand. The World Wide Web has that name for a reason. We are speaking to the world. The engagement must be wide. A web emphasizes strength through intricate, complex interconnectedness. Nothing could be less suited to combative, controlled information than a network of communication that reaches everywhere there is a voice to be heard. It is not the Tower of Babel but the ivory tower that is to be feared. The tower of many languages was simply a story made to frighten us back into our own little tribes so that leaders could control us. Now we have www.babelfish.com.

The third development that cries out for a more robust manner of thought revolves around a series of medical discoveries. Researchers who focus on the way we think – from neuroscience, psychiatry, psychology, philosophy, and a number of other areas – have fundamentally altered our understanding of how the mind works. Over the past few decades no other area of research in the academy has come as far (you may wonder about information technology, but for a variety of reasons that has been largely a private-sector revolution).

We now know more about *knowing* than ever before. One area that seems particularly interesting is our species' struggle with the remnants of our ancient brains. Often referred to as the reptilian brain, the *triune brain* that was first proposed by Paul MacLean in the early 1990s points to our ongoing struggle with the "fight or flight" reflex that kept us safe when we were living out in the open.[33] It seems that we are particularly susceptible to threats to our security. When we feel under attack, our adrenal glands release a powerful chemical into our bloodstream to assist us in both fighting and fleeing. To support these two protective features, our bodies move blood into our larger muscle groups. This transformation allows us to hit harder and run faster than we could have only a few seconds earlier. It also means that the blood that had been feeding our brains has been reallocated.

What all of this means is that when we apply a model of intellectual engagement based on attack and parry, we are initiating a process that drains our brains of blood just at the time we most need to be able to think. To think most clearly, we need to feel safe. Not surprisingly, creativity experts continually talk about finding ways to encourage us to take bigger risks, to "not be afraid to fail," to work better together, in order to explore new vistas of human existence where all people have value.

Biology tells us that models of thought based on aggression will almost certainly stimulate the oldest, most linear, and most violent parts of our brains. Today's politicians, advertisers, and spin doctors know this science well and have connected it to ancient Platonic teachings. As a consequence, we are being bombarded with messages about things we should fear in order to make us behave in ways that please our masters.

In this chapter I have taken us on a lightning-quick ride through history. One last thought experiment: ask yourself how much change has actually occurred in the world of critical thinking. Our world has changed in myriad ways, yet our operating system for engaging with it has not. That system is still being used to frighten us, and to attack foes, and it is almost always a gateway drug to the potent form of character assassination known as *ad hominem* attack. Listen to the violent rants of our politicians. If you are like me, these professional combatants do not anger me. Instead they look like shadows. They look like older forms of life, no longer living in the present, no longer looking to the future or offering vision. They look as though they should be propped up for display in museums of natural history.

We deserve better. The time has come for us to stop fighting fire with fire – indeed, to stop fighting entirely – and instead begin sitting around the fire only when it provides just enough warmth and light for us to see one another's faces while sharing ideas.

One final note before we proceed. If you are not convinced by any of the above, how about this: Why not question critical thinking just for the sake of internal consistency? If critical thought is always and everywhere committed to seeing all sides of an issue, then surely the system itself should be subject to the same requirements.

In 399 BCE, Socrates tipped back a cup of hemlock and escaped the world of critical thought for good, but he left us trapped inside, and we have been suffocating ever since.

Chapter 3

A Hitch or Two

Polemic, Violence, and the Case for Critical Thinking

Toward the end of his autobiography *Hitch 22,* Christopher Hitchens includes a section on drinking. Hitchens was famous for the amount of alcohol he could consume without negatively impacting his ability to work. Hitchens explains his "rules for drinking," which include half a bottle of wine for lunch, more for dinner, but nothing strong afterwards. To this he adds further rules and then advice for young imbibers. He points out that one of his close friends reminded him that those who have rules for drinking are usually alcoholics. Hitchens is quite clear that while he may have some small tendencies, he is no alcoholic. I want to give him the benefit of the doubt, but it is true that those who spend a great deal of time talking about their rules for consumption of alcohol and ensuring us that they are not alcoholics seem to have a more serious relationship with strong waters than those who do not.

When one begins to study the history of critical thought and examines its texts from the past to the present, an interesting trend becomes evident that puts me in mind of Hitchens's assertions about tippling. Those who write about critical thinking and those who practise the art of critical thought almost always feel the need to tell their audience what critical thinking is *not.* Critical thinking is not – they tell us – a negative way of looking at the world. The word *critical* in the formula does not mean what we think it means or what the dictionaries say it means.

In *Hamlet,* the young prince is presented with a dilemma. Stuck with one foot in the old world of revenge and one in the new world of Christian forgiveness, he struggles to decide what to do about the evidence he has that this uncle has killed his father and seduced his mother. Following good creative practice, he decides that the only way to the truth is through the staging of a play. When his mother Gertrude sees on stage a series of events resembling her own life, her son asks her how she likes the play. Her reply – "The lady doth protest too much, methinks" – has become famous as an example of the same type of denial we encounter in life of the alcoholic and the critical thinker.

Correcting misrepresentations of our selves or some other state of being is a part of life. Needing to make the correction on an ongoing basis, however, is more than likely an inverted admission of guilt. What if critical thinking is – or at least partly is – an inherently negative approach to life? Given that English is what is known as a use-based language, rather than a rules-based language, it is likely that if we are continually fighting against the understanding of a word, then we are also fighting against some aspect of truth. In English, if the vast majority of the users of the language believe *critical* to be a pejorative – even after thousands of years of education to the contrary – perhaps it is time we accept the verdict.

Given that a use-based language reflects what words mean to the people using that language, some weight must be given to what those people understand words to mean. We have all come through an educational system based on the critical thinking model, so we should expect that if the program is working our dictionaries should reflect at least some of what critical thinking is supposed to mean.

When we open the *Oxford English Dictionary,* we find that the vast majority of definitions provided for *critical, criticism,* and *critical thinking* are negative. Indeed, the only positive definitions seem to be recording people's attempts to argue that critical thinking *is* positive. Let's examine some of the definitions:

1. Critic:
   a. one who pronounces judgment on any thing or person;
   b. the art or action of criticizing;
   c. relating to a crisis of disease;
2. Critical: given to judging;
3. Criticism:
   a. the action of criticizing, or passing judgment upon the qualities or merits of anything; esp. the passing of unfavourable judgment; fault-finding, censure;

b. the art of estimating the qualities and character of literary or artistic work; the function or work of a critic;

c. the critical science which deals with the text, character, composition, and origin of literary documents, esp. those of the Old and New Testaments;

d. an act of criticizing; a critical remark, comment; a critical essay, critique;

e. a nice point or distinction, a minute particular, a nicety; a subtlety; in bad sense, a quibble.

When we look at definitions of criticism or critical thinking in texts that tell us why it is so important for us all to become critical thinkers, we find long discussions of why what we think about critical thinking is wrong. Does it not seem strange that after 2,500 years we still believe that critical thinking is judgmental and negative? And why is it that the cure for our widespread acceptance of this definition is supposedly *more* criticism, fed to us by the chief producers of the form, whose identities rely on its existence?

No writer added more new words to the English dictionary than Shakespeare. Within our tradition he is held up as the most important figure in the English Renaissance and as one of the greatest thinkers the world has known. He was writing at a time when there was no organized grammar, no organized spelling, and no organized criticism of his work. The newly introduced printing presses were chugging along creating new documents without rules of grammar or spelling, and people seemed to be able to read them, yet today we teach Shakespeare as if he somehow supported the regimented engagement with culture that we promote in our schools.

Perhaps more important than the way critical thinking and rules-based pedagogy limit creativity is the way these seem to promote a language of violence. A detailed study of critical works uncovers a long list of words that seem to connect to critical thinking's history of fight-or-flight responses. We are said to *interrogate* and *investigate* texts. Why are these tactics necessary? What in you might make you wish to conduct interrogations? Is it the good part of you? Are we up against a foe that has information vital to national security? What about *dissecting* or *anatomizing* texts? Is there some thought disease for which we think we can find a cure?

When an author puts forward a play, poem, story, or essay, why should we greet it with such hostility? Is not the act of speaking a form of contribution? In all but a few cases, would not a language of joining, collaborating, and meeting the speaker be more hospitable? Just who do we think we are fighting, and to what end? Is it not simply rude to begin all conversations with the language of suspicion and violence?

This linguistic militarism comes from critical thinking's long-standing connection to the status quo. It is experts in critical thought who draw the writs that close theatres, censor books, and bring citizens before tribunals to answer for crimes related to the expression of ideas. Have we ever seen a dissident called forward to share his or her ideas openly? No, of course not. When the police come calling it is always critical thinkers who have sent them, for critical thought is deeply committed to aggression. To attack a text is not the same as to attack a body, but the two very often go together. Indeed, a solid critical argument is usually the precursor to the repealing of laws that protect citizens. It is here that we see the difference between critical thinking and dissent. The former is conservative; the latter tries to expand our horizons through the discussion of alternative propositions.

Critical thinking does not have the force of ideas behind it, yet it seems to attract us at a deep level, and it is always trying to persuade us of its importance. We come by these critical tendencies honestly. Perhaps the most famous of all forms of intellectual engagement in the academic tradition is the debate. The Oxford Union is a world-famous institution committed to the pursuit of ideas.[1] It has also offered a great deal of entertainment by using thought as a competitive, spectator sport.

I admit to having enjoyed a few victories of this type myself. In one of my lowest academic moments, I once made a fellow student weep and run out of the room when I savaged him for ridiculing the work of James Joyce. He was taking potshots at someone I regarded as an important writer, and instead of engaging his ideas, I attacked. Of course, it is just this type of behaviour that is at the heart of critical thinking. Even when dressed up it always smacks of that type of velvet-hammer cruelty one expects of clerics or private school dons in the English novels of the nineteenth century. No matter how we disguise it, it reeks of violence.

I cried when Christopher Hitchens died, and tears still come to my eyes when I think of his passing. He was, it has to be said, one of the greatest critical thinkers of our age. No less a figure than Salman Rushdie proposed that as a debater, he was superior to Cicero.[2] It is said that not only did he never lose a debate; he never ceded a single point. I find this highly unlikely, given the sheer amount of debate he engaged in during his career, but it is clear that he was a unique talent with a powerful intellect.

Those of us who feel that Hitchens's commitment to freedom of speech and support for various unpopular ideas made him a type of intellectual hero can still admit that in some debates his ruthlessness could make us squirm. In one particularly gruesome event, he was pitted against his own brother, who during the course of events lamented having agreed to the debate and promised never to be so foolish again.[3] Hitchens was a brilliant orator and a genuine devotee of ideas, but his vicious side always embarrassed me and somehow made me feel diminished. To me, he was far more powerful when being open and celebratory, as demonstrated in the marvellous recording he made of his autobiography.

Here we must face a very serious question. Could it be that in order to face the questions that Hitchens addressed, one must be willing to take up the weapons of criticism and use them just long enough to lay low the tyrants, torturers, and sacred cows of our world? I find myself wishing I could say no, but the answer may not be so simple. It would be disingenuous of me to recruit Hitchens to the creative side, for he was ever the critic, but I suggest that the power of his examples owed as much to his love of freedom and ideas as it did to his need to fight for his beliefs.

While I believe that his position at times took him into a dark place that was no longer primarily driven by ideas, I can at the same time entertain the notion that he was using powerful weapons in order to tackle issues that were many times larger than he. In most if not all cases, the originators of the ideas he attacked had used far more violence than he brought to the conversation. Is Christopher Hitchens then the patron saint of critical thinking? Is he the proof that we must train thinkers to fight for ideas and to open doors to darkened rooms to ensure the light gets in?

Yes and no.

Hitchens, like many other leaders in the world of ideas, was committed to a *type* of critical thinking, but not the diminished form that pervades our educational system today. In fact, his career was fuelled in part by the lack of informed dialogue from the academy, a lack resulting from the demographics of universities. Today, there are fewer professors in relation to students, and those professors are aging. This is not a happy circumstance at a time of revolutionary technological change. Hitchens was a gadfly – a self-appointed regulator at a time when few in the academy were fighting for their ideas in the public sphere. Others, such as Susan Sontag,[4] Steven Pinker,[5] Cornel West,[6] Marshall McLuhan,[7] bell hooks,[8] Noam Chomsky,[9] Francis Fukuyama,[10] Jane Jacobs, Edward Said, and Judith Butler, attest to the need to blend academic and public life in order to live the life of the mind.

More on that in a moment ...

Early adopters of creativity as a primary operator for the workplace promoted "brainstorming" and other models of creative sharing. These practices can be quite illuminating but are not entirely satisfactory. They are designed to bring about an explosion of ideas, but in themselves they are not sufficient to generate productive work – thus, the popular conception of this type of work as fluff, as mere entertainment. It sparks ideas but fails to harness them in any meaningful way. Recalling our definition of creativity, these approaches feed newness but lack value.

When creativity experts look for examples of success, one of their heroes tends to be the late Steve Jobs, whose career with Apple, Pixar, and some other smaller ventures is the stuff of legend. Most academics and students are aware of his now famous commencement address at Stanford.[11] He is a cult hero of the creative movement, but he does not fit with the fluffy model of brainstorming.

Many artistic people like Jobs because of his attention to aesthetics; business leaders like him because of his business acumen. But the real engine behind his success was his mode of work. Jobs famously led intense sessions of critique that were designed to keep his company at the cutting edge of thinking. His ruthless behaviour during these meetings – details of which have been recounted by a number of friends and former colleagues – seems to clash with his public image as a warm and lovable figure launching new products each year at events staged almost as rock concerts.

"Real artists ship."[12]

Jobs's most famous quote referred to the idea that to be a genuine creative it was not enough to merely come up with ideas – you had to go to the next step and realize the potential of those ideas. You had to find value, which in Jobs's view was measured in consumer impact. To find that value, you had to endure Apple's infamous working sessions. Various authors who have studied the creative process point to Jobs's approach – and similar ones at Google, 3M, and Procter & Gamble – as proof that brainstorming must be combined with critical thinking if it is to produce anything of substance. So, if the artist is to "ship," she must first endure critical attack.

The survival argument is merely the critical tradition attempting to maintain its claim over innovation and productivity. What Jobs and his fellows were doing, and what I believe Hitchens was doing, was offering *constructive criticism*. The term will be familiar to you, dear reader, and I suggest a simple reason why. Critical thought is a violent, reductive system, but it has shown itself to have many positive elements. Those elements are almost always found in what has come to be known as *constructive criticism*. The fact that the formulation seems to be a contradiction in terms – a kind of "building destruction" – attests to the fundamentally damaging nature of purely critical thought.

When I meet people who lobby for the importance of critical thinking, they are almost always actually talking about *constructive criticism* (most of the others are defending *critical theory*, which is an entirely different topic).

Here we must ask ourselves: If critical thinking actually is giving us something positive, something useful, something contributory, why then do we need to add the word "constructive" as a modifier when we wish to convey that the criticism we are about to share will be helpful? The reason is that critical thinking alone contains no requirement to offer anything positive. So thoroughgoing is its destructive force that the term *constructive* needs to be added as a promise of non-violent engagement at best or as compensation for the amount of suffering you are about to inflict.

Think about the moment when this type of criticism is offered. When we ask someone if we can "offer some criticism," they invariably recoil a bit, waiting for the ensuing attack. We attempt to calm them, and bring civility back to the engagement by promising that what we will offer will be in the name of something positive. It will help to construct – to build rather than destroy. The term is entirely positive, unless we change the tone of its delivery to a sarcastic or more purely critical one, in which case the listener prepares for an even more vicious attack, realizing that the critic is judging not only our work but also our person and will now hold forth on how we might better live our lives in order to suit them. If critical thinking is a form of violence, constructive criticism that is not actually constructive is like domestic violence – it is not just pure aggression, but aggression in the place where hospitality has been promised, and it is carried out in breach of that contract.

In real terms, this means that when we are engaging with our fellows in such a way that we are working toward a positive end, constructive criticism is essential. Unfortunately, those who espouse a universal form of critical thinking as the model for all education believe that all criticism is somehow inherently a contribution to life, when in fact the vast majority of it is destructive. Steve Jobs's passionate criticisms in the morning sessions at Pixar and Apple led to products the entire team produced. The mutual benefit component of this work meant there was an overall positive connotation to the work. Not so much, however, that workers would have endured it without the massive salaries that offset the pain and suffering. It is important to note that even with those salaries, many brilliant minds quit, refusing to endure such criticism. If we want creative people to be creative, we must promise them safety and comfort to a point, or else we must compensate them adequately for their pain and suffering. But is not the point of education to alleviate or address suffering? Surely it is not to cause it.

In a lifetime of political and cultural commentary, Hitchens was playing a role he felt he shared with a long line of intellectuals, chief among them George Orwell.[13] Hitchens never stopped reminding us that he was never Orwell's equal, but he remained committed to sharing his hero's commitment to speaking truth to power on behalf of those who are suffering.[14] When he went over the line of decorum, he claimed to be fighting fire with fire. Thus, his attacks on Mother Teresa[15] were carried out with a knowledge of the crimes of the Catholic Church, and his attack on Bill Clinton[16] with the knowledge of the lives lost in Rwanda because of mistakes in that man's presidency, and when he got around to attacking God and organized religion, he did so in response to what he saw as a long line of atrocities.[17] We are free to decide how much or how little we agree with his positions, but I think we can admit that he seemed to believe firmly in the positions he espoused.

Some will observe that his was a special type of critical thinking – a purely destructive, but destructive in the same way that a surgeon's knife or chemotherapy is destructive. That is, it is carried out in the name of eliminating something of great danger. For me, the mind that devotes itself to the pursuit of the truth and that maintains that commitment regardless of the consequences is deeply committed to the creative powers in our world. But to commit to that type of attack has its costs. As Nietzsche warned, we become the enemy we fight.[18] It is not hard to hear the increasing bitterness in Hitchens's critique the longer he remained in the arena. It is this tone that made his work critical thinking and not political dissent. But he certainly had his moment.

When the *fatwā* against Salman Rushdie was announced, very few academics had the courage to support him. Such was – and is – the fear of radical groups claiming to be inspired by Islam around the world that very few had the courage to support freedom of speech. Hitchens's behaviour and his writings in support of Rushdie are among the most important statements made in the last half of the twentieth century in defence of the *agora*.[19] They may well be on par with the greatest statements made on the subject. Susan Sontag – a public intellectual like Hitchens – was there as well, but those who worked under the system of critical thought in the rarefied air of tenured protection for speech were nearly all silent.[20] It is a point of great embarrassment for the academy and raises questions about the ability of critical thinking to address real issues.

Hitchens got a little too angry for my taste sometimes – so much so that it made me uncomfortable. Just as when his brother Peter lamented the beating he received at his brother's hands in their debate, there were times when his attacks seemed to be little more than verbal battery. We must ask if there were times when he worked himself into a rage and was no longer in his right mind. Perhaps this is the dark side of availing oneself of the sharper edges of the potent art of critical thinking.

In cooler tones, Hitchens always affirmed the superiority of art to criticism, of the creative over the negative, and he was quite clear that his place in the world was to be a contrarian. He wished he had been given the gifts of Auden, Amis, and Rushdie, but since he did not, he would fight to the death to protect their right to speak and be heard. His strength came from the depth of his engagement with poetry, art, and music.[71] That his tactics sometimes became acerbic demonstrates the costs one incurs when allowing oneself to operate in the critical thinking mode. It cannot help but taint even the best of our thinking with the flavours of violence.

When we study Hitchens or Jobs, are we making the argument that the ends justify the means? Again, the answer is yes and no.

Creativity experts tend to point out that some form of criticism must be brought out at the end of brainstorming or experimental sessions to help focus the work. Certainly, given the stress of working for Apple or of risking your life to get a story (as Hitchens did on a number of occasions), serious remuneration will be required to entice the individual to engage with the process. In the end, most people would say that Steve Jobs and Christopher Hitchens were successful in their fields. They caused some suffering, but the positive far outweighed the negative by the measures they applied to themselves.

But that is not the point.

In the case of these two well-known thinkers, harsh criticism sometimes played a role in creative practice. The broader lesson, though, relates to how criticism is used. Creative work is *primary* – it is the governing mode of operation. Critical – that is, *constructively* critical – work comes after the fact and in far less volume. Over and over we find that individuals or groups that are consistently innovative operate with creativity at the heart of their work and with critical work kept as a fine-tuning device whose use must include a payoff in terms of the final delivery of work or at least some kind of development in craft.

The balance between the critical and the creative is at the heart of my proposal. Why not place creative, innovative, and inventive thought at the heart of the university and dramatically scale back critical thinking? We need to re-examine why we feel we should be loading students up with critical thinking they don't want, and neither do their employers nor the rest of the world. The only other possible reason to offer critical thinking as a way of engaging is that the students enjoy it. But they don't. Critical thinking does not make us happy; it has exactly the opposite effect.

We need to place the creative at the heart of everything we do, say, and teach at the university. This would completely reboot our schools and allow us to become dynamic institutions of ideas rather than the conservative, dolorous islands that we have been left with after millennia of intellectualized complaint. Students should leave our campuses having been trained in innovative, creative, inventive thought – not just a highly developed ability to find one thing wrong with everything they see.

I predict that within a very short time neuroscience is going to show us that training in negative thought is damaging our brains. Some studies have already suggested this and have demonstrated correlations, but we are early in the process. Looked at this way, critical thinking is a form of abuse. It cannot help but be abusive – its history is one of dominance, repression, and combat. The only time we really need it anymore is as a tool for fighting its own monsters – as a "fight fire with fire" homeopathy that can help cure us of the narrow, limited modality that is holding us back from a broader perspective and more congenial engagement with others.

What level of responsibility do we bear to our students if we take them in as creative, passionate thinkers and turn them into specialists in abstract hyper-thought that focuses only on finding problems? Where is the development of the vast network of new thought that arrives on our campuses each September? Are we any better than our religious forebears, who had a vested interest in controlling the minds of their young charges for specific socio-political ends?

Performance experts often point out that Shakespeare, Bill Gates, and Albert Einstein all rejected school and instead set out to revolutionize the world. Is it any wonder that so many of our most inventive students flee our classrooms? The question is *why*. Should we not be incubators of the next big idea? Of course we should – and we must. It is no one's fault – we were all brought up in this old-fashioned mode of thinking that is no longer serving our interests. We will have to work hard to change, but it is essential that we do so. Critical thinking takes so much more than it gives. So why not stop? Critical thinking has had its chance to prove itself, and all it has brought is systemic misery. Universities should be places of joy, so why not return them to their natural state?

Pedagogy experts from Ken Robinson and bell hooks to Roger Schank talk of the need to completely restructure education.[22] For generations, we have talked about reform and complained about the diminishing returns of an education. We are now at the point that funding bodies such as the Thiel Scholarship are offering money to students to avoid university and go straight into research and development. And why shouldn't they? Our campuses are being run by a skeleton staff of the oldest professoriate in history at a time when the Information Revolution is pushing wave after wave of innovation through the public and private sectors. In the twenty-first century, only the academy is dragging its heels, and that is because we refuse to let go of the past even though it is killing us. How can this be? The answer is clear. We are suffering from a disease, and that disease has a name.

Nostalgia.

Some campuses are debating whether computing devices should be banned from classes. I have done numerous interviews and call-in shows where people have suggested that classrooms use no computers at all. Suggestions like these come from a place of fear. Times of great change generate trepidation, but banning technology from the classroom? Students will not come to class if we educate them for the nineteenth century when they are going to be graduating – with record levels of debt, by the way – into a world of networked, global interactions. We do not need computers and phones *all* of the time, but they need to be on *some* of the time.

On campuses around the world, scholars are asking themselves why so many of the academy's traditional disciplines are losing students. Our long slide into nihilism in the traditional disciplines has led to a migration into professional degrees. Long seen as more focused on job training than pure education, faculties such as business and engineering continue to grow as more traditional research areas collapse. But it would be wrong to think we are serving our professional students as best we can. We are failing all of our students, but in different ways.

In the medical and professional fields, the call for creativity is as loud as anywhere else on campus. I first became interested in this area when I realized that the vast majority of creativity research was being conducted by people in disciplines outside those fields traditionally associated with creative work. Governments, businesses, and administrators are all looking for ways to prepare people for the new world ahead. On campuses, creativity research is being done in faculties whose primary concern is not normally the creative. While humanists remain tethered to critical thinking, professional schools and social scientists are pouring time and money into creativity. And where are the students going? They are following programs that are committed to discovery. Good for them.

In the long run, we all have a responsibility to begin working in ways that incentivize discovery and help us escape the pointless negativity of critical thinking. Debate that is based on winners and losers is a thing of the past. The debate is over, and we all lost.

At the core of the university, pure research in the arts and science has been tainted by our commitment to critical rather than creative thinking. Part of the response to this has been the retreat of service courses from the centre of the university to the safety of individual faculties. We now have separate writing, research, and methods classes in almost every area, with little if any interaction among students. The professional faculties do not want their students studying in courses that do nothing but teach them to criticize, and who can blame them? The slow migration away from the creative and toward the abstract, critical model on our campuses has turned our institutions into factories of complaint. Students have voted on this with their feet and left the centre of campus, and they are unlikely to return unless we make dramatic changes. Evolution does not reward the fastest or the strongest – it rewards those who adapt. How have you adapted to the changes in our world?

Creativity, innovation, and discovery are as necessary for engineers, accountants, economists, chemists, and doctors as they are for dancers, musicians, artists, and actors. And the best way to enhance discovery is by creating and maintaining a diverse *agora* – a meeting place for public discussion. We need conversation among all of our students based on the notion that by working together we are building the body of knowledge. We need to teach that working together allows us to discover more than we would if we worked alone. By working together, we acquire skills in networked intelligence that will serve us for the rest of our lives. This is also a fundamentally more humane approach to teaching, learning, and research.

If the university becomes a model of collaborative research, our graduates will be far more likely to understand the benefits of working together when assigned group projects in the working world. Imagine that a cohort of students experienced education that rewarded the innovative, creative, and collaborative nature of inquiry. Then imagine those same students later finding themselves in different political parties. Perhaps their default mode of operation would not be pointless attack, but rather cooperation. How can we expect productive cooperation when our educational system does everything it can to punish it? When we withdraw into separate disciplines or support on-campus rivalries between programs, we build disciplinary rather than intellectual allegiance. The word university comes from a root meaning "the whole," as in the *whole* of society. As long as we are merely a collection of faculties, we cannot hope to achieve the universality that names our endeavour. Placing creativity at the heart of the university will bring us together again to support our task.

But what of Hitchens? What of the great battles that must be fought against the enemies of thought? Are there not times when we need to respond directly to pernicious ideas in order to stop them before they cause harm?

These questions are of central importance. While I was writing the first draft of this book, a group of people in Texas challenged what they called critical thought in an attempt to promote a literal reading of the Bible. If I thought that my argument would in any way support this type of thinking,

I would delete all my files immediately. These individuals said they were attacking critical thinking, but my guess is that this is not all they were attacking. Indeed, I would suggest that educational systems based on critical thinking (which means almost all of our schools) are what promote this type of us-versus-them thinking in the first place. What they were doing *was* critical thinking. We should remember that it was religious schools that shaped the model of critical thinking we continue to use. So while fundamentalists from around the world might wish to target critical thinkers, I humbly suggest that they are using critical thinking to do so. Critical thinking as an operating system has shown itself perfectly suited to violent fundamentalism throughout history. However, the focus of this book is not on individual debates, but rather on the binary discursive system that frames them.

When people who support creative, open, and contributory thinking disagree with fundamentalist approaches to education, it is because those approaches encourage near dictatorial control over the information being transmitted to students. Typically, such approaches call for students to be fed one particular explanation for the world at the expense of other narratives. It follows that proponents of these controls are not speaking in favour of religion; they are speaking in favour of *their* religion. More than that, they are speaking about how their religion should be imposed on people. They want to win. This type of approach is dogma, not faith. To promote such narrow definitions of education, the combatants use critical thinking. Critical thinking trains us to break arguments apart, find weaknesses, and attack. It offers the simplest way to reject new ideas, and that is why it will always be the best friend of tyrants, no matter how benevolent they advertise themselves to be.

Christopher Hitchens knew these tactics, and he understood the importance of the debates he chose to enter. As someone with a natural gift for argument who had spent years honing his craft, he wanted to express his skills in the Olympics of the critical world – by opposing the biggest, strongest opponents he could find. But in so doing, he had to make sacrifices. His lapses into aggressive behaviour were one price he had to pay.

Hitchens's good friend and fellow combatant Richard Dawkins has made a similar bargain. In his most recent writings, Dawkins argues that we need to redirect our interest in myth and magic toward a deeper appreciation for science, which, he says, brings to light the "magic of reality."[23] His approach is similar to the one Hitchens chose – a full-out attack on ignorance on the largest stage possible – but we have to ask what is sacrificed when we allow ourselves to resort to violent language. Why are the arguments always win/lose?

Everywhere in the world, we find myths that explain how our world works. Every civilization – there are no exceptions – has its stories of how life began and why we are here. These stories, when understood as metaphors, enable us to think beyond what we are capable of when we only consider a reality that is easy to describe. Stories such as these can stretch our minds. If taken literally, they pose the same risks as any religious dogma, but they are not inherently corrupt, and it is too easy to dismiss them as such.

But before we pass judgment on people who delude themselves with friends and facts that support ideas they already hold, we should recognize that when we speak about these people we are speaking about ourselves. The human mind is predisposed to recognize patterns in the world that lead us away from what is true and toward what we want to believe. In our best moments, we are capable of improving our ability to think, but the very systems we use to understand our world seem to betray us. Recognizing that is essential to the creative endeavour.

Our brains, like other physical entities, prefer to use the least amount of energy possible. Thus, we think through a variety of issues along the way, and after we have spent enough time on them, we pin them to the walls of our minds. We do not constantly re-evaluate the information in our world; we simply do not have time. As a result, on an ongoing basis we take down these old, dusty opinions and reuse them when something in our lives leads us into that part of our neural net.

We know from years of research that our conscious minds triage information so that we are not overwhelmed. Our unconscious deals with some of the excess, but it is inflected by old opinions that we keep running – like outmoded software – because we have not had the time, the desire, or the information to update them. As a consequence, our world view is continually being corrupted by old data. Add to that the fact that our minds are inherently bad at evaluating statistical reality and we find ourselves constantly in a tricky negotiation with the world outside our heads.

At a societal level, this same practice plays out. A major book or discovery becomes the central way of explaining a historical event or a set of phenomena until a better explanation comes along. Or does it? Of course it does eventually, but what usually happens is that the new idea or discovery does not get adopted because there is inertia around the old idea. We are committed to it and we do not want to let it go. Paradigms take time to shift.

In the academy, this cognitive distortion lies at the heart of the way we work. We are trained as critical thinkers who must defend our ideas. Imagine the reaction of the leading critical thinkers when a new idea emerges that proves that the work that has been their identity-giving truth is wrong.

They do everything in their power to destroy the threat to their egos, and they use their years of critical training in the attack. Creativity encourages new ideas; criticism stops them cold. If we were trained not to attach ourselves to ideas, but instead to be constantly adapting to new ones, then no new idea could ever threaten us in such a fundamental way.

And herein lies the dark connection to *ad hominem* attack that so often rears its ugly head in the realm of critical thinking.

By allowing critical thought to degrade, we have turned ourselves into beings whose identities are connected to particular sets of ideas. We have commoditized thought so strongly that our very lives are at stake when someone offers a better way to explain the world. There is no area of research that has not been hampered in its progress by eminent scholars working to prevent change. They have to protect their careers, their livelihoods, and their identities by sticking to old ideas and killing the new ones. But remember, this is not about "them," it is about "us." We all do this, and we will continue to do so. Creativity merely offers us a better way to engage with our natural challenges.

When we link thought so directly to identity, *ad hominem* attack becomes incredibly powerful. People are always asking why the public is so obsessed with character issues when the political issues of the day are so much more important. The reason is that the public has been trained to think in ways that cause them to associate ideas with identity – ways that are inherently destructive. So candidates for office, candidates for jobs, and candidates for friendship work to smooth out opinions and ideas into homogenized offerings that will not activate the critical defence mechanisms that keep these from being accepted.

Which brings us to a very important question: If we are biologically and culturally predisposed to misinterpret the world and trust old ideas over new ones, do we not need people like Christopher Hitchens and Richard Dawkins to criticize our assumptions in order to ensure progress? Again, the answer is yes and no. Hitchens and Dawkins can both be described as secular extremists whose chief enemies are religious extremists. It may well be that that is what is necessary today so that we can grasp what the parameters of discussion should be. But I would argue that at their best, Dawkins and Hitchens are not being critics. The same can be said for those they oppose.

I have already pointed out that Hitchens provided new ideas and new ways of thinking that were often creative rather than critical. I would place Dawkins in this same category. I have also noted that Hitchens sometimes lost focus and gave in to anger. Here too I would place Dawkins with Hitchens. But this does not capture most of what these two, and others like them, achieved in their efforts to champion unpopular people and ideas.

At about the same time that modern critical thinking was getting started in the ancient world, another school was being founded – that of the Cynics,[24] who believed in finding the best life by distrusting all received and imposed knowledge. Taken to its extreme, Cynicism could be as flawed as any other approach, but at its core it remained committed to the idea that we must continually test the ideas we have come to accept as truth. The Cynics knew that we always become lazy in our thinking and that if we are to be truly happy we have to be vigilant about remaining open to the next idea. The original Cynics thus shared a commitment to what, at its best, we today call dissent.

Dawkins and Hitchens on their good days have more in common with the ancient Cynics than with critical thinkers. Like the Cynics, they pose questions in the name of improving the human condition. Critical thinkers, by contrast, pose questions in order to *complain* about the human condition. Critical thinking does not require us to remain open to new ideas, only to attack old ones. When Hitchens became too aggressive, when his arguments descended into elaborate taunting of his opponents, he veered into critical thinking. Dawkins is prone to the same error, as we all are, having been raised in a world where critical thinking is the dominant mode. We cannot help but breathe it in the air and drink it in the water.

Another point: if all systems must be modified over time, then we must find ways to speak truth to power. The political realm seems to be the key forum for this type of discussion, but it extends to all areas of society.

The thought experiment I am asking you to engage in suggests that we need not spend time attacking every bad idea – better that we share ideas until better ones replace the ones that are failing. We should grow the grass rather than attack the weeds. As a theory, this is fine, but what should we do when we share our ideas and no one listens? And what if the reason we are fighting is that a powerful figure is limiting our ability to speak? The leaders of countries sometimes force their ideas on their citizens even when those ideas seem abhorrent to most of the people they are impacting. How are we to respond to this?

We must recognize that as we attempt to move past critical thinking, we will encounter some very serious obstacles. I believe having moved toward a more open, creative, and loving approach on university campuses, we will bring about change in all of society over time. My solution is not a quick fix. It offers a quick implementation strategy and some fast results, but it will require much more time to replace the old, violent models that currently underpin civilization. Violence is easier than love, though love is far more powerful.

The idea that violence must sometimes be used to stop violence has a long history in our world. So does the misuse of arguments for "just wars." The answer is not to fight against fighting, but rather to accept a more loving approach to thought.

No dictator kills his people in order to bring suffering on himself. No corporation cheats in order to bring pain upon itself. We pursue our happiness by whatever means we think will work. An educational system that demonstrates the benefits of a creative approach will alter the goals we are pursuing.

The experts who debated what to do about Rwanda were all trained in critical thinking. The experts who discuss Darfur are all experts in critical thinking. The experts who discuss Syria are all experts in critical thinking. Where is debate getting us? Are UN resolutions anything more than antiquated calls for debate?

If our leaders were educated to believe that solutions were the goal, and not attacks, defences, and victories, then they would be predisposed to find ways to act. If we trained all students to view critical quagmires as negligence, then our negotiators would no longer begin with lists of non-negotiable items. Creativity makes no room for the non-negotiable. Great ideas require no protection other than the room to breathe and the right to live.

An academy that trains all of its students in all of its disciplines to believe that our primary commitment is to continually engage with new ideas will transform itself so that it supports innovation, entrepreneurship, and creativity instead of merely cataloguing complaints. The person without ideas should be offered further education. Nothing fuels the mind like research. The committee member with no new suggestions should be dismissed. The cynic who questions systemic paralysis should be welcomed, while those who do nothing but complain should be politely shown the door and not invited back.

Complaint without contribution is violence. And we are all violent.

In the famous "To be, or not to be" soliloquy, Shakespeare's Hamlet wonders whether he should accept the role of avenger. He stands between two worlds. The first one operates on revenge, the second requires him to contemplate forgiveness and the idea that it is not for individuals to mete out justice. We have struggled with these issues for centuries. It is now time for us to accept that the combative verbal art known as critical thinking has its roots in revenge. We protect those with whom we agree, and we defend against those with whom we disagree. In a never-ending cycle of violence, we go around and around accomplishing little except the prolongation of pain. For Hamlet, the only way out was death. For Shakespeare, the solution was simple: his work foregrounded justice, mercy, and creativity. Let us follow Hamlet and only take up the sword of critical thinking when there is no other way forward. In the meantime, let us turn to the creative path to see what it has to offer. As Christopher Hitchens said, it was art that freed his mind and school that taught him to fight. We should change that.

Chapter 4

We Can't Go On Together (with Suspicious Minds)

Diamonds are funny things. Everyone agrees that they are beautiful to look at. They even have some industrial uses in drill bits and saw blades. But they are not actually very valuable, because they just are not that rare. Those in charge of the world's production, refining, and sale of diamonds have found ways to artificially inflate their value – ways that have succeeded so well that the imposed value of diamonds is high enough that every year, many people lose their lives mining and selling them.

Critical thinking is a bit like the diamond trade. No one doubts that it is brilliant on the surface and that it is very good at cutting into things, but we have falsely inflated its value in order to maintain cultural capital in our educational institutions. In a similar fashion, when you question either the diamond trade or the retail market for critical thinkers you are in for some heated discussions. The problem with cleaning up the diamond trade is that we are deeply attached to the illusion. We have marked those stones as somehow related to our highest expressions of love and have spent billions on them, so no one wants to admit they are only worth a fraction of what we say they are. Perhaps it is the same with critical thinking. It seems to be getting tougher to sell university education these days, and we think that if we give up the notion that we are in possession of advanced mental tactics that can be taught for a price, then maybe we will lose value in the marketplace of ideas.

The emotions that drive the diamond market are not necessarily bad, and the public seems comfortable with the ongoing narrative about the diamond trade, but we should have *all* the information before we make up our minds. In the area of critical thinking, people have more options. The growing interest in creative thinking can be seen in every corner of the academy. This interest extends across geographic boundaries and is now as hot a topic in India and China as it is in Canada and the United States.

The market for critical thinking is collapsing, with departments that traditionally linked themselves to its instruction losing numbers while other parts of the university grow. The fastest-growing areas all have programs that connect to words like innovation, entrepreneurship, invention, and creativity. This is quite exciting for those of us who are interested in the world of creative thought; however, it is important that those in the disciplines whose focus is linked directly to creative work be part of the discussion.

Around the world, people continue to ask for diamonds. More and more of them are being mined, and every major city has dozens of retailers offering them. The same cannot be said for critical thinking: no one is asking for more of it. No business is saying, "What we need is more criticism – let's look at this issue critically." No government office is saying, "What we need is a more critical approach – who do we have that is a critical thinker?" We do not look to our politicians, our educators, or any of the industries that serve us and ask for more critical people. In fact, it turns out that we would like significantly *less* of it.

When we look behind the scenes, we find that today the world of critical thinking is a bursting bubble. There will always be value in it, but it currently holds an artificially high value that needs to be adjusted down. Meanwhile, creative thinking is enjoying increasing demand and is poised to replace its more linear cousin as the mode of thought of greatest benefit to most of us. To engage most fully with our talents as individuals and as citizens of a global community, we need to engage with open, contributory modes of thinking and working. I call this *loving* thinking, and it involves working from a position that begins in hope rather than in suspicion.

Elvis Presley had one of his biggest hits with a song penned by Mark James titled "Suspicious Minds." That song, big, bold, and beautiful in that Las Vegas style that Presley grew into, warns us that "we can't go on together ... with suspicious minds." It cautions all lovers that you cannot be in a fulfilling relationship when you begin from a place of suspicion. In Shakespeare's *Othello,* act 3, scene 3, the hero declares: "Excellent wretch! Perdition catch my soul, / But I do love thee! and when I love thee not, /

Chaos is come again." Othello suspects early and learns late that when we are gripped by suspicion we lose all harmony and hope of rest.

What both Elvis and Othello knew is something we should come to grips with if we hope to find a better way of working for the twenty-first century. Critical thinking instructs us to treat all incoming information as if it were coming from a hostile witness in a jury trial.

We begin from a place of suspicion and pry open every seam in every statement to check for weapons of deceit. The result is – as Nietzsche warned – that we become the enemy we are fighting. Or the enemy we *think* we are fighting.

If beauty is in the eye of the beholder, then so too is ugliness, and our relentless pursuit, not of the truth, but of any attempt to deceive us, causes us to see conspiracy everywhere. The alternative I propose is *loving* thinking. In this model we begin by giving the author the benefit of the doubt. We start with the assumption that most people are simply trying to communicate with us and that their attempts to do so indicate not hostility but hospitable engagement – they are inviting us to *join* something, are not bullying us into believing ideas that could harm us.

Imagine a child who is about start school. Her ideas about what she would like to do often relate to the things she sees in front of her – sometimes through the media, but very often pulled from daily life. Thus, children often dream about working for the fire department or driving a garbage truck. The sociologist Pierre Bourdieu reminds us that children are governed by the world in which they find themselves.[1] Their dreams are made of the bits and pieces of the lives they are living in this moment. Nature has equipped us with the spirit of inquiry, but we need education to help us build on our dreams.

When we enter school we are full of dreams about what we want to do, and those dreams are cast in positive terms. Those who study creativity are fond of the Picasso quote, "We are all born artists; the trick is to remain one." Education experts pick up on this and ask how our school systems are failing us: Why do we seem to be quashing dreams rather than nurturing them?

Our horizons expand as we learn more about the world and about our lives and as we gather more materials for constructing our dreams. The problem is not in the materials educators provide but in how they deliver them. We are teaching students to think critically so that by the time they graduate from university, it is a benchmark of success to be able to call oneself a critical thinker. As a consequence, students know more, but they also dream less.

But wait. Has anyone ever *wanted* to become a critical thinker? If we gave people a choice, would they *ask* to become critical thinkers? And if we asked parents whether they wanted their children to become critical or creative thinkers, which would they choose? And perhaps most important of all – when did we begin to feel that it was okay for our universities to teach us how to think? Shouldn't the point of university be to free our minds so that we think for ourselves rather than to train us all to think the same way?

The repercussions of critical thinking are visible everywhere. The financiers who nearly bankrupted the world economy were trained as critical thinkers. They were expert competitors who knew how to present their ideas in the most persuasive ways possible. They also knew how to fend off competing arguments when their practices were questioned. If community rather than rhetorical rivalry were at the centre of our education, perhaps they would have felt a greater need to respond directly to those who questioned the house of cards they were building.

Governments certainly do not need more critical thinkers. In Canada where I live, every year, big yellow school buses roll up to the parliament buildings in Ottawa. The children on the field trip step down with their backpacks and brown-bag lunches and are given an orientation session. Part of that session involves the teachers and organizers instructing the children to behave themselves while in the viewing area. Another involves a detailed explanation of why the people they see will be fighting, yelling, and insulting one another. The children are told that this is how high-level politics is conducted – that this is what civilized governance looks like.

Stop right there.

What if the children's instincts are correct? Do some adults have the same feeling? Of course they do – opinions of politicians and the way they conduct themselves are at their lowest in history. It is embarrassing for our children to see people behave in this way, and it is irresponsible to deny the feelings we have when we witness this carnage. What they see is an example of the worst kind of behaviour. In any classroom, that behaviour would earn them a correction. What these children are witnessing is the operation of critical thinking as it has developed in our political system.

In Canada we actually call these people "the foreign affairs critic," or the "environment critic." Do we ever hear these people offer creative contributions that could improve the lives of the citizens they represent? Of course not – no matter what the government says, the critic disagrees. So bad is this sort of gridlock that governments in the United States seem unable to pass any kind of legislation. They would rather the population suffered than cede the point on any issue. The European Union, the African Union, and the Arab League are similarly locked in destructive battles. What we have now is government run on critical thinking. The good news is that people have had enough and want change. The bad news is that the people who have a vested interest in the old ways are willing to do anything to block change. How could they do anything else? They have spent their lives fighting not for society but for a win at any cost.

Is it not strange that governments, which contend they represent the will of the people, have a position known as the whip, whose job it is to ensure that everyone in the party supports the message they are told to support? As with school trips to the seat of power, students who study political science or political philosophy initially see the truth behind the word whip, but over time are groomed to believe it is a normal part of democratic functioning.

Governments today are being challenged more than ever before to engage with one another. Globalization is placing huge demands on nations to work together. A glance at the UN Security Council shows us just how difficult working together can be. How might we best prepare our future leaders to negotiate with one another over contested lands, differing belief systems, and conflicting economic interests? Is it best to be suspicious of everyone else in the world, or might we build a better future by following leaders whose creative capacities have been developed? For the early Greeks the answer was simple – we are best prepared to serve society if we move past our critical skills and embrace a more creative, contributory model that allows us to *care* for ourselves in ways that enable us to best serve society.

When we consider the results of an educational system governed by criticism, it quickly becomes apparent that our current machinery is broken. Why don't we start at the top? In two recent federal elections (Canada and the United States), two candidates stood out for the way in which they presented themselves. Jack Layton in Canada and Barack Obama in the United States tapped into a different kind of energy. Layton passed away shortly after he was elected, and Obama has been attacked for not sticking to his message, but it is their messages that interest me here. Their campaigns highlighted exhaustion with old ways of doing politics and a desire for change. It is doubtful that either could have done what he promised, given the logjam of competitive politics, but it is telling that both were elected for having a vision of something better.

Both candidates made a case for positive dialogue. Both connected with voters who were Internet savvy. Both were unlikely heroes who shocked the political world with their success. People of all stripes are tired of the way our politicians work. It seems that all candidates for office try to portray themselves as anti-establishment, but this nihilistic position is merely the other side of the critical thinking model. It still relies on an "us versus them" mentality; it still seeks to isolate problems, describe them, and find people to blame. In this model, everyone is defined in negative terms – that is, they come to have meaning for us not through ideas but because of who they oppose, and how.

Obama and Layton changed all of that. Or at least, they promised they would.

Forget about what their policies were or whether you agreed with their particular ideas; instead, look at how they connected with people. We have been told that campaigns must run negative ads in order to win. As a result, we have come to expect these critical messages that cost tens of millions of dollars every election cycle. How did we become so apathetic that we would accept this travesty? The answer is, we did not, but our system makes it seem as if we had. Part of us will always respond to ads that target our instinctive response to attack, but our better selves follow ideas. It turns out that what wins you votes is a new message that talks about the future. Layton did not win, but he did secure the largest increase in votes in his party's history – and at a time when many thought his party was nearly defunct.

Barack Obama became famous for his speeches about visionary, inclusive ideas. His victory challenged many long-held beliefs about politics. His connection to the electorate was more granular and grassroots than had been thought possible. By utilizing technology, his fundraising and get-out-the-vote campaigns were able to tap into the public imagination. Individuals felt empowered, and Americans were thrilled to be able to vote for ideas rather than anger. Years earlier, on the other side of the political spectrum, actor-turned-politician Ronald Reagan had been able to motivate voters from both sides of the aisle by expressing a positive vision of the future. While many feel that Reagan's message was not as unifying as Obama's, it came at a time when the United States had lost faith in itself. His vision projected over the horizon, and his commitment to a pathway to the future engaged huge portions of the electorate. He did not have the benefit of the Internet, but his training as an actor meant he was expert in the technology of his time – television.

For both Layton and Obama, the Digital Revolution made all the difference. Both also brought out the youth vote – a group that had been written off by traditional parties in almost all countries other than those challenged by revolutions, which are often the product of young people without hope for the future. As many young people voted in the last American election as seniors did, and that was when most millennials were not yet eligible to vote. Engaging them will transform politics.

I hope you will permit me a brief mention of a local example.

A recent mayoral election in the city where I live offers a good example of the power of creative, open, loving work. Calgary, Alberta, has a reputation for being the most conservative big city in Canada. When the mayoral campaign began, several established names came forward, and everyone in our city believed that alderman Ric McIver, who was known as "Dr. No" for his record of opposing almost every motion before the council, had a lock on the job. His values fit well with a city perceived to be monolithically committed to traditional conservatism.

Naheed Nenshi, a self-declared devotee of creativity expert Richard Florida,[2] got into the race polling in the low single digits. To the credit of all involved, the national and then international media became interested in what was described as "a campaign in full sentences." All of the top candidates seemed to be in it to promote their ideas for the city's future. There were no negative ads and no underhanded tricks – at least, none by the candidates themselves (the media launched some unsavoury attacks). When Nenshi won, it seemed almost unreal. Critics from other cities and other countries celebrated the city's decision to elect a candidate of ideas who put creativity at the forefront of his policy. Well after the election, he continued to enjoy the highest approval rating of any mayor in the country; he has often been described as the most popular politician in Canada. People are shocked that this creativity guru could be elected in a conservative town. But he is a different kind of politician, for a different populace. Calgary is not what people thought it was – rather, it was a city ready for a change.

The lesson is clear: contrary to what we are told repeatedly by those who seek to achieve and hold power, ideas are more powerful than hatred and fear. Creativity trumps criticism. Love really is the best route to political influence. It is one thing to talk about running better campaigns and expecting better behaviour from our leaders, but in these cases we are actually seeing examples. As with Obama and Layton, Nenshi used information technology to share his message. He had far less money than most of the other candidates, but he was able to make up for that with a positive message that appealed across the political spectrum and that brought out the all-important youth vote. As with Obama, once his message connected, online donations began rolling in to support the campaign.

We are discussing these examples simply to indicate the hunger for a politics of vision. These candidates were more complicated than any theory, and we cannot fully capture their performances when we reduce them to metaphors for the shift toward more creative politics. What they do tell us is that overall, people want something different. It will take time for us to truly move to a more creative politics because the system in which these figures find themselves is run by people trained in the combative style known as critical thinking.

Obama, Layton, and Nenshi found support for positive politics in the online electorate. So before we move to a different field of social organization, let us pause and consider Wikileaks, one of the most controversial groups in the info-political realm. This small organization states that it is committed to social change through access to information. Shortly after it released a wave of documents revealing the communications of international diplomats, governments set out to discredit the group and its leader Julian Assange in any way they could. The most disturbing aspect of this was the uniform message that came from our leaders through the media: governments must be able to withhold massive amounts of information from the public in order to run the world. Why do we accept this assertion with so few questions? The message here is "We have to lie to you to keep you safe, and anyone who tries to stop us must be imprisoned. We must have elites who perform all our decision making." How is this different from the clerics who told medieval parishioners they could not be trusted to read the Bible they were told they had to follow?

In Plato's ideal society, only those at the top would be privy to all information, so he would not have approved of Wikileaks. Of course, he was not designing a real democracy. No political system in the world disseminates more self-serving propaganda than the United States, yet when it comes to actual governance, the American approach to information is avuncular at best. And herein lies an important political message: creative work requires freedom of information, and critical thinking promotes the control of information and the discrediting of perceived opponents. Ask yourself – would you not feel safer if you were in twenty-four-hour-a-day communication with the citizens of Iran and China instead of leaving it up to our leaders?

When did we give our leaders permission to lie to us and withhold information? At least Plato made it clear that in his ideal world, philosopher kings would be our superiors. Our superiors take this power upon themselves while telling us we are free. We are not anywhere near free if our masters interpret the truth before we see it. That type of politics is what we get when we train future leaders in critical thinking rather than creative, open, loving engagement. They are trained to say anything in order to win. But before we become too judgmental, remember that it is we who train them and then reward this behaviour. Perhaps we do need to maintain tiers of information access, but we should have citizen monitoring of all that material at every level if we want to be able to tell ourselves we are living in a democracy.

So, when it comes to politics, is anyone anywhere asking for more criticism? For more suspicion? For more attacks, more violence, more fighting? No. People around the world want loving, open communication, but it is in the vested interest of a tiny ruling class to keep information from the population. Let us be clear, this is not a conspiracy. This state is the result of a world run by citizens who are trained in suspicion, fear, and violence.

In Plato's ideal city, the true heroes of society are those who work for the city and serve their fellow citizens. In this regard we have experienced a major shift. We no longer view our civil service as something that is there to serve us – to enrich society and ensure its smooth running. It is an entirely acceptable mode of attack to complain about civil servants. Part of the mandate of these groups is that they have little access to the media; thus, they make excellent straw men for those who seek influence through aggressive words. After all, if we have been trained to use language as a means of attack, what better target than a group of victims who are not allowed to fight back? The easiest fight to win is the one where the opponent cannot return our blows.

Hypocritical politicians pay lip service to the military and to so-called first responders, but our firefighters, soldiers, police, health-care workers, and teachers work for lower pay in our societies than almost any other group, while those who work with critical language and who do not produce anything tangible control most of the wealth and enjoy most of the prestige. Here, Plato would criticize us, for in his ideal society the highest aim we could have would be to progress through training in critical mind to arrive at caring mind in order to better serve one's neighbours. For him, service was the highest calling and rhetoric was empty by definition. Strangely, our corruption of his structure has inverted his ideal order.

Perhaps the only sector of society that moves more quickly than the political cycle is the world of business. We live in the age of the market economy, and all of its strengths and weaknesses are on grand display. Far too often, those who call out loudest for competition are in fact working the system as hard as they can to cheat their way to success. It is embarrassing to see because it reminds us of our basest nature. Creative work in the world of business leads to innovation, entrepreneurship, and invention, whereas in a world in which all students are trained in critical thinking, defeating other people is often the unstated goal. Wealth is relative, and if the only way we can succeed in society is by defeating others, then the more people we throw under the bus, the more successful we will be.

Fortunately, some global business leaders are modelling another way of working. No one accuses Bill Gates or Warren Buffet of being a shrinking violet in the world of business, but their positions on philanthropy have restored faith in the best aspects of our system. And here again we find a connection to creativity. The position on philanthropy that is being adopted by many in the business community came out of a movement started in Silicon Valley. The creative class there began making fortunes in IT. Their interests have fundamentally reshaped the world of work. When they looked at what they could do with their considerable fortunes, they asked new questions about philanthropy. Frustrated with what they saw as broken governments, corrupt business models, and a lack of international will, they developed creative ways to address the world's problems. While the thieves at Enron were bankrupting thousands and the lobbyists on Capitol Hill were presenting critical arguments that asserted ideas such as "money is speech" and "a corporation is a person," these figures were reminding us that it is not business that is bad – the problem is those who cheat, lie, and steal to gain dominance. A model of thinking that tells us to win arguments at any cost and to treat all others with suspicion directly supports this type of behaviour. Indeed, we must all shoulder some of the responsibility for the global market collapse. It was, after all, merely a collapse of a series of well-made arguments that had no bearing on the real world. As long as we live in an economy that must grow continually at the expense of the majority, we will create monsters that prey on us. But the role of inspiration through the exploration of new ideas should not be left to the market. That is not its role.

Our main focus in this book is the university, so let us turn our attention to how it operates. Enrolment in disciplines whose primary focus is critical thinking is down and continues to fall. Nowhere is this more apparent than in English departments. Beginning in the late twentieth century, they got out of the business of literature and writing in order to focus more on the mass production of criticism. For many years, English departments had two great strengths. First, they were the place that students could go to study stories, poems, and plays and how they were created. A highly skilled professoriate took students through a sampling of writing and celebrated the best that research had uncovered. Given that we all grow up hearing stories, these courses were a natural draw. The full-year survey course often acted as a modern day *agora* where students from all departments and all backgrounds could come to engage with creative works that examined the foundational ideas in our intellectual tradition. The lists of books to which they were exposed were continually updated, but the discussion was similar on campuses around the globe, and, as a result, a conversation was engaged across large regions of the world.

The other great strength of English departments was that they taught writing. Given their primary subject matter, it only made sense that they would be the ones to instruct students from across the campus in how to express themselves in English. Eventually, though, the teaching of literature and writing came to be seen as menial labour and was cut back and assigned to sessional teachers or graduate students. Elite professors focused on critical thinking and published in the area. Abstract criticism was equated with research, while formal explorations of reading and writing in English were seen as teaching. If you were to walk down the hallway of an English department during this period you would almost never hear literature or creative writing being read out loud, but you could be absolutely certain that you would hear criticism.

The largest market for first-order critical thinking emerged from this change in English departments (as well as in all other campus departments) after what was known as the "linguistic turn." A group of critics called the Russian formalists once asserted famously that we must "make it strange" – that is, we must find ways to draw new attention to ideas that are taken for granted.[3] I hope we can "make strange" the insane assumption that English departments should exist without a commitment to the teaching of reading and writing.

The worst of this period is now over, and English departments everywhere are migrating back to the familiar ground of English as a coherent field of study. The primary reason is that no one really wanted what the old guard was selling. A type of sadomasochism had seemed to overtake us as we stopped reading and writing and committed ourselves instead to the rhetoric of attack. Those in the academy now speak openly of the "hermeneutics of suspicion" and its after-effects.[4] Different writers approach this term in different ways, but in all cases it refers to a model of approaching texts with critical rather than creative thinking. Tellingly, the change came not from the workings of critical thought but from our fellow citizens. People simply lost interest in what the critical thinkers were saying. We are now at the moment of complete collapse, and not surprisingly, those who are desperate to defend the status quo are launching loud and well-crafted messages of fear and hatred.

What critical thinkers of all stripes have forgotten is that there is a force far greater than all of their fear and violence: the voice of the people. Young people not sufficiently indoctrinated into the politics of the critical mind are demanding more from their engagement with government, business, and academe. Of course, student movements have always been dangerous for those who would oppress us, but now, with the advent of information technology that allows networking in hitherto unimaginable ways, change – *big* change – is approaching quickly.

On campus we already see the change. Administrators, researchers, staff, and students are demanding that creativity play a larger role on campus. No longer satisfied with the kind of nihilism that comes with critical models, people today want action, and action requires doing something rather than endlessly listing problems and their outcomes. Governments are encouraging students to pursue interdisciplinary and practical fields. Part of this is because that governments tend to think in the short term and are trying to address employment issues, but part of it is that no one needs students trained in the old critical thinking model. We no longer want problem solvers who spend their lives looking for problems. If all you look for is problems, that is all you will find. Particularly if your job is problem solving. It is hard for us to admit our job is pointless.

A recent article in *Forbes Magazine* listed the three questions that define every job interview:[5] (1) Can you do the job? (2) Will you love the job? and (3) Can we handle working with you? This article perfectly captures the same hiring rule that many people have talked about on university campuses over the last few years. There, this question is called "the photocopier question." Roughly, it goes like this: Can you handle meeting this person at the photocopier every day for the next ten years?

Assuming then that those in the position to offer someone a job are all sharing the same general background – qualifications, passion, and relationship skills – what model will serve us best? We can already see signs of the resurgence of creative interests on campuses. In those same English departments that gave up on reading and writing we are encountering a return to aesthetics, to formalism, and to creative writing. Almost certainly, this will lead to a renewal of the study of English. High-level, abstract criticism will also benefit as more readers and writers pursue the formal studies necessary to ground the best theoretical work.

Today's students face a rapidly changing world, and they understand that many of the old promises no longer hold true. Moreover, the fiscal reality of education is coming closer to their lives as student debt soars. These students have access to more information than any generation in history, and they are using it to make better choices and to demand change. In North America, the National Survey of Student Engagement (NSSE) has shown repeatedly that students want classes where they leave behind traditional disciplines and work in new ways with students from across the campus. When institutions respond to the needs of students, they will be rewarded. When they stay mired in the past, they will lose enrolment.

What can we possibly offer to students who can now receive free online lectures from Harvard, MIT, and Yale? What we can offer is education in the present – in a room with real people having a discussion rooted in the moment. The Information Age has removed barriers to information that have been in place in every other age – including those periods that designed and modified university education. Students no longer need someone to stand at the front of the room and deliver data. Rote lectures are quite simply an inferior delivery mechanism; however, engaged work done live in a room with teachers and students will always be a primary method of intellectual engagement. As with Socrates and his teaching in the street, there is power in personal communication. Of course, you had better not be a modern-day Thrasymachus, or you might just be excluded from the discussion. In the current age we call these people trolls – because they troll online discussion merely to complain – and the movement to eliminate them from discussion boards is massive. People are not interested in bitter students any more than they are interested in grumpy teachers.

Organizations representing university professors routinely criticize the use of teaching evaluations to judge the quality of work among the professoriate. Why? The argument against teaching evaluations is that they cause teachers to work harder to be popular, which shifts their focus away from more serious academic work. What if there is an error embedded in that assumption? What if, because of the culture of critical thinking, we have come to think of the serious academic as someone who is angry, suspicious, and tempestuous? If that were the case, these figures would almost certainly be in trouble on those evaluations. But what if the professor being evaluated was creative, passionate, and open? Would that person not end up being more effective and – dare I say it – more popular? I often think of a professor I had at McGill during my undergraduate years. He read from detailed notes for each lecture he delivered. He never looked up, he kept the room dim and only had a small lamp on his papers, and he never veered from his prepared notes. The class was extraordinary. Why? His ideas were bold and continually evolving. Students hung on every word. You could hear a pin drop in the room during his pauses, and people were always there on time so as not to miss a moment. My guess is that when you started reading that description of the class you thought I was perhaps going to use this as an example of a tired old classroom model, but the fact is that as long at the ideas are fresh, creative, and engaging, students will be hungry for them. No amount of edutainment would have drawn us away from those quiet, methodical lectures. To be popular is not to be an entertainer – to be popular is to be a person of vision who connects with students. Our whole system is founded on Socrates, Plato, and Aristotle, all of whom competed on the streets of their city like buskers of information. Popular might also mean brilliant.

Student evaluations are not perfect, but when did we begin to take it for granted that if the people we teach do not like what we are doing that those opinions should not be factored into our performance reviews? It is in our interest to do so because we are all now being evaluated online as well as on campus. Like it or not, the discussion about our work is live. Moreover, these types of evaluations are early warnings for the direction of enrolment. Disinterested students in undergraduate programs do not pursue graduate study or professional work and will not keep the advancement of knowledge going. Show me a passionate undergrad and I will show you a future leader, whether in business, government, or academe. Every institution I have ever attended or worked at had professors with quirky presentation styles that would drive everyone away if it were not for the power of their ideas. Ideas are more valuable than flash, and it is time we stopped blaming students if they do not like what we are saying. After all, what if they are right?

A key challenge to any shift toward the creative is the system of tenure. No academic in her or his right mind would argue against tenure, but we need to re-evaluate it. Tenure, which was fought for long and hard, has become an elaborate disincentive program. At its best, it is used to protect the production of ideas that might be unpalatable to the powers that be. As such, it is an absolute must for a creative society. But when was the last time you saw tenure supporting that kind of work? Why not take a minute and write down all of the cases of which you are aware? Where was the academic outcry over the misinformation that took the world into Iraq? Where were the academics when atrocities against women were uncovered in the world of the Taliban and other like-minded regimes? Where are the work actions to challenge the system of indentured servitude that now reigns supreme on university campuses, where sessionals, adjuncts, and students are assigned most of the heavy lifting? Tenure is not being used to protect new ideas; it is being used to sustain barren old ones. When powerful companies or governments want to silence academics, they do – and they do it regularly. Where is the outrage? Where are the marches for social justice?

But the outrage does come. It comes when anyone suggests that senior faculty might not be able to maintain their lifelong jobs or that they will not receive yet another pay step while most of the work on campuses is shouldered by labourers who are unprotected by tenure and who have no hope of attaining it. Here is one of the greatest and most fundamental injustices in our society, and the very people who claim tenure in order that their ideas may benefit our society perpetuate that injustice. We simply must do better.

A creative workplace requires freedom of ideas and freedom of expression, but only a very few are afforded those protections. If those few are not using them to help their former and present students receive just treatment in the workplace, how likely are they to put these powers to use for the betterment of society? Again, we have a situation where those who generate criticism are rewarded and those who actually work are punished. For life.

We should tenure creativity, not criticism. We need new ideas, new ways of thinking, and new ways forward, not the inherently regressive system we currently have. We often hear crazy talk show hosts calling the academy liberal, but nothing could be further from the truth – the professors of today are ultraconservative in the most literal way at a time when most of the world is caught in a maelstrom of progress.

When we look for areas of dynamism in the university, we find them where faculty members connect to their communities: in business leaders who lecture and work, engineers who build and teach, doctors who heal and research, writers who publish and mentor. They are everywhere, but they are not being given the type of support that would best serve a creatively driven world. We need to incentivize creation and penalize obstructionism. Change must come – we have a fundamental responsibility to innovate, to discover, to assist our world. The university ought to be the engine of ideas in society, and it must take that role seriously or be dismantled. If we do not embrace that role, we will lose our position little by little to think tanks and laboratories, which will lure our colleagues away with the only promise that matters to true academics – the pursuit of the next new idea.

Of course, the university is already being dismantled. There is no better way to see behind the wizard's curtain than to have non-stop information flowing in and around our campuses. Creativity thrives in an environment of open access to information, and we live at the time of the greatest opening in history. Just as when Plato first argued to control information, dark powers are working hard to lock down the Internet and control information. Open access is a dangerous thing for critical thinkers – it is far too democratic, far too wild, and far too much fun to work well with linear, combative models of social and intellectual interaction. Let us all hope it helps bring down the global totalitarian forces of information control.

We live at a time of great debate over the organization of our social interactions. Many tie everything to financial markets and to the world of buying and selling. The idea that free markets of goods are necessary in order to achieve true freedom is not ambitious enough – what we need is a free market of *ideas*. Mere possessions are too paltry a thing to remain at the centre of our lives. Once we stop training ourselves to believe we should always suspect one another and that each argument is to be won or lost, we will experience a revolution in every part of our lives. Having freed ourselves of the need to defeat others, we will no longer require so much conspicuous consumption. Wealth is not necessarily a bad thing, but it is beneath us as a primary goal. Human flourishing in a broader conception should be our aim.[6]

Over the past several decades, a movement called positive psychology has taken hold in some parts of the academy.[7] Breaking with tradition, those working in this field are asking some powerful, simple, and new questions. Why do we spend so much time and money on problems and almost no effort on developing the positive aspects of life? For generations we have focused on diseases of the mind and body rather than on growing, nurturing, and developing the positive sides of ourselves. Adherents of positive psychology teach courses on happiness, love, and joy. They examine the ways our lives could be improved in the short and long term by growing the good rather than complaining about the bad.

Tellingly, those who work on positive subjects were met with ferocious attack by the world of critical thought. Critical thinking works best when we focus on the world as a corrupt and paltry place that is out to deceive us at every turn. A new breed of scholars is saying "enough." Let us study our successes, our joys, our triumphs, and begin to move society forward not with fear and hatred but with love and compassion. Study after study has shown us that happy people are healthier, smarter, and more productive. Why do we continue to study misery when almost all the evidence urges us to change? The commitment to critical thinking is so deep that we would rather keep bashing our heads against the wall so that we can talk about how good it will feel when we stop.

The first happiness class that was offered at Harvard was packed. It became the most popular class on that campus. When we offered a happiness class at the University of Calgary, a similar thing happened. Students will follow the move toward a more positive engagement with life. We already know they are abandoning nihilism in droves, so we must ask: What if we taught critical thinking and no one showed up?

In a rapidly changing world that is increasingly global, and in which we now know that human life can be improved with a little attention to the way we live our lives, should it surprise us that students want a new way? And should we not want that way as well? Or is it the case that some of us have stock in misery and do not wish it to lose its value?

Happiness experts agree that materialism is anathema for human flourishing. Yes, we all need a certain level of wealth to achieve our peak happiness, but that barrier is surprisingly low – around $60,000 a year adjusted for inflation. Valuable work and social relationships are what bring us true happiness. The experts have certain areas where they disagree, but on wealth and happiness they are uniformly convinced – you need to do things that matter, and you need to be socially connected. You need to complain less and be more positive if you want improvement mentally, physically, and socially.

What would an education committed to *those* goals look like?

Critical thinking teaches us to be suspicious of others, to view conversation in a combative fashion. Its chief mode of production is judgment. Does that sound like a path to meaningful work and positive social interactions? Creative work is committed to making new things that have value. Does that not sound more like meaningful work? Creative thinking is committed to welcoming others with open and loving arms. Does that not sound like it could lead to meaningful relationships?

Let us take this one step further. Do a thought experiment – think of the most critical people you know. Are they happy? Do you envy the lives they are living? Now think of the most productive, influential people in your field. Are they joyful? Are they connected, are they making new things that have value? Where do you fit in the experiment?

We need to begin to take responsibility for what we are teaching our students and what we are feeding society. If science now tells us that isolation and a negative approach to life actually makes us unhappy, less intelligent, and unhealthy, why are we doing this to ourselves and to others? Could a case be made that we are harming our students, our staff, and our colleagues? We may be able to demand the right to self-harm, but should we be allowed to hurt others in the name of our ideology?

Remember that the form of critical thinking we work with now was inherited from a religious tradition that contended that enforced suffering would help us get into heaven. If you believe that, then perhaps you should continue to pursue a life governed by critical thought. But perhaps you feel – as I do – that there may have been an error in that thinking and that in fact we have a responsibility to do the best we can with whatever time and gifts we have been given. What if we have an ethical obligation to re-evaluate our commitment to critical thinking?

I do not know of anyone who wants more criticism in their life who would not benefit from a little more light rather than more hostility, fear, and combat. If we rediscover the commitment to both sides of academic training with which the ancient Greeks started our system of education, we might help foster a new renaissance. This renaissance would be based on a love of learning, a love of self and other, and a commitment to make things better in this world. *Loving* thinking and not critical thinking.

Critical thinking has a vested interest in suffering. By continually telling us to distrust one another and ourselves and to reconcile ourselves with a fallen world, critical thought paves the way for an empty, consumerist society. Without the joy of meaningful work and close social bonds, we turn to drugs and alcohol, to food, to possessions, and to verbal and physical attack to distract us from the pain of emptiness in our lives. Worse still, given its oppositional nature, critical thinking always makes the world's woes someone else's fault. Thus, the grumpy old critic can sit back and do nothing to help the world because everyone else is responsible.

Fortunately, it seems that our natural state is one of joy. When information flows freely and we can hear our fellow human beings and ourselves, we become more creative and more integrated. Not surprisingly, organizations and groups that have an interest in controlling us through the mechanisms of pain and fear do not like open access to information. Knowledge and information are power, and the longer we can be kept in the dark the longer we can be kept as slaves. Without information we can be told to hate one another, to kill one another in wars we did not start, and to starve one another with unjust economic practices. None of us – unless we were genuine sociopaths – would not help others if we truly knew their stories. But to get that story, we have to be willing to listen and they have to be willing to talk – and that state of being can never come from a suspicious approach to the world.

As you see, diamonds are a funny thing. They are not actually that valuable. They require us to agree upon a lie. So powerful, so indivisible are the stones and the story that people are losing their lives for them right now.

Chapter 5

An Immodest Proposal

Let's Replace Critical Thinking with Creative, Loving, Open-Source Thought

Imagine university campuses governed by creativity as the primary mode of operation. Imagine that incentives directly promoted collaborative work that is always seeking the next idea, solution, or creation. Imagine a community run with open information that is shared freely in order to continually contribute to ever-widening discussions among everyone on campus, on all campuses, and in communities around the world. Now, think of the university that is closest to you. Does it feel, creative, loving, and open? Most if not all of the time, the answer will be no. Our universities were founded as extensions of churches that had chosen to follow a path of self-mortification, worldly suffering, subservience, and controlled information. Traces of those early commitments continue to govern our academic world.

In *Either/Or*, Søren Kierkegaard provides a powerful image of the artist's role. The artist, he writes, is born with a physical difference in the way the structure of his mouth is formed.[1] This physical alteration causes the sounds of pain to be transformed so that when the individual cries out in agony, his fellow citizens hear them as beautiful music. According to Kierkegaard, society has an interest in keeping the artist in pain. We have a similar condition on our university campuses. The image of the tortured genius patrolling the halls of the ivory tower, head in hands and pondering the woes of the world, is a deeply held stereotype. It is an illusion that must be eliminated.

We now know that happier people score better on all tests of intelligence and productivity. So why do we still support that old image of mental achievement? That agonized figure in the beret does not have a superior intellect; he may actually have a medical condition for which we should show compassion. We should stop infusing our young with an illusion that causes them to court angst, depression, apathy, and nihilism. We should also free our academics to pursue a more joyful existence. They are afforded the opportunity to live the life of the mind, which is a rare gift. In the words of the economist/philosopher Jane Jacobs, they are blessed because they are given "the time to think." We should revel in that fact. Of course, Jacobs was able to pursue her joyful and influential career because she rejected academe and its agonizing navel gazing and instead went on to change the way the world works.[2] She remains one of the most influential thinkers in urban design, economics, and creativity, and she is taught in universities around the world, and she knew she would never have been able to achieve what she did if she had to work in the current system.

How many of us looked forward to university only to find that it was just an extension of the worst parts of high school? Where was the passion? Where was the joy of learning? Where was the celebration of the fact that human beings have incredible potential that we can actively develop? These are not dreams – they are the desires that wave after wave of students come to campus with, only to have them squelched by the world of critical thought. We bond with our fellow students over our ability to endure suffering. School is no longer about poetry, projects, and adventure; it is a second-order engagement with problems. Our professional magazines and societies talk almost exclusively of problems and the fact that things are constantly getting worse.

Consider the following quote: "The children now love luxury. They have bad manners, contempt for authority; they show disrespect to their elders.... They no longer rise when elders enter the room. They contradict their parents, chatter before company, gobble up dainties at the table, cross their legs, and are tyrants over their teachers." Those words are usually attributed to Socrates and are hauled out each year as an inside joke among academics. It reminds us that we have been complaining about students for as long as we have been teaching in this way. In fact, the attribution is less than clear, but it is fascinating that we feel the need to tell ourselves this joke over and over. Who "doth protest too much" now?

The good news is that universities are changing. A revolution in education is evident everywhere on university campuses. The area in which we have the most room to grow is the one governed by faculty. Famously, Jean-François Lyotard predicted that the role of professor would soon be obsolete.[3] He made that prediction several decades ago. Could it be that the time-honoured position of the professor has come to an end? I do not think so. Information experts will always be required, but certainly the role we play needs to change dramatically.

The critical thinking model is perfectly suited for the old process of education. Pedagogy experts call this model the "sage on the stage."[4] For years, experts have pointed out the problems created by the power dynamic inherent in this relationship, but that relationship is no longer the biggest problem. The major issue with this type of structure is that it cannot compete with a student who has a smartphone. Information is constantly being updated, and if you think you can stand at the front of a room and impart pearls of wisdom, you had better be prepared for a question from a student in the lecture hall who has just found a more recent article than the one you are discussing and who wants to know what you think about the new developments in your field of which you were unaware when you wrote your lecture last week.

For years we have taken it for granted that all of us at the university should teach critical thinking to our students. Why? What does this instruction do for them? There were times in the past when it allowed for a meticulous engagement with relevant scholarship and prepared students for the type of linear debate they might encounter in the Toastmasters or at an academic conference, but that type of thinking no longer prevails in the world in which we live. The students in our classrooms now grew up in the age of IT, and they know how to find information instantly. They know how to access more information on a topic in a few moments than we could have reasonably done in a weekend at a good research library.

Information today is dynamic, and our engagement with it is no longer structured in long streams that we can slowly evaluate and categorize. How can we live in a world of nearly infinite information? Any approach that attempts to apply linear, evaluative models such as the one promoted by critical thinking is doomed to fail. I suggest that we need to engage information and change our approach to one that is based on creative, open, and loving modes of work. In this chapter we look at the philosophical change that needs to happen; in the next, I provide some concrete examples of what we can do right away.

In her article "Unlearning How to Teach," Erica McWilliam brings together the leading figures in education, philosophy, and creativity to demonstrate that the way we are working now must change.[5] As she points out, universities have been very slow to adapt to the changes that have revolutionized the world in the last few decades. To be fair, universities were never designed to change quickly, but it is clear that our current transition is such that if we do not modernize we may well see the demise of universities entirely.

No one is more connected to the idea of a new educational system than Sir Ken Robinson.[6] His three TED talks have sparked thousands of further explorations of our engagement with information and learning in the twenty-first century. After he called for profound changes to our educational practice in his first talk – which has been viewed more than 25 million times – his second address asserted that we do not need reform or even radical change, but that we *will* need to completely dismantle the educational system and rebuild it to suit the demands of the world.

Robinson's idea is popular among thinkers in the fields of learning, performance, productivity, and creativity. Richard Florida, Daniel Pink, and Malcolm Gladwell all look at the way we are functioning in universities and find us hopelessly outdated and reluctant to respond.[7] Leaders in education, business, and government are all looking for the workers and leaders of the future. Most feel, like Robinson, that a tectonic shift in education and training is required.

My suggestion is at once bolder and simpler than Robinson's. For Robinson, the problem with our system is that it is connected to the Industrial Revolution's interest in product-based thinking. He is correct, but I would add that the industrial-age model of education is only a minor symptom of a larger problem. The demands of factories and of product-based societies were merely an extension of our long commitment to an aggressive, winner-take-all strategy in thinking and learning. We taught in such a way that as long as our society emphasized competition, production, and control from above, our methods shone. This model worked particularly well when universities were being founded in the Middle Ages; it was challenged during the technologically supported creativity of the Renaissance; it reasserted its dominance during the Industrial Revolution.

Our problem is far older and far deeper than the Industrial Revolution. Our problem is that we are too hard on ourselves. That may sound trite, but it is true. We have become fascinated with personal and interpersonal attack and the idea that an intellectually rich life must necessarily be dour and severe. The dominant position held by the politics of cognitive suffering means that our universities are no longer centres of discovery and have instead become small cities of irrelevant bickering. Some point to revolutionary moments when universities became the agents of great social change, but a quick examination of those periods will show that those movements had nothing to do with the universities and everything to do with groups of organizers and activists who resisted the institution and the values for which they stood and continue to stand. In the same way, when we encounter individuals whose contributions have shone out from university campuses, they uniformly speak of working outside, around, or against the system in order to make the discoveries for which they become famous. Well-known examples are found in the biographies of Steve Jobs and Bill Gates, but there are thousands of similar stories.[8] Jobs and Gates made huge contributions to education, yet both spoke openly about the ways in which the educational system did not work for them at all.

The way to fundamentally change the university, and thus our way of thinking as we progress toward different professions, is to alter the blood that pumps through its veins. That will require a foundational change. For this, we will need to re-evaluate our university missions, our faculty goals, and our departmental motives. If we begin to view our central goal as connected to creative engagement, everything on our campuses will change.

Consider how students arrive on a university campus. In the years before they show up, they have been pushed to fit into one or another path that will lead to university. As Ken Robinson so rightly points out, the highest goal of education currently is university entrance.[9] Once there, the pinnacle of success is to become a professor. The entire path is couched in critical thought and a threat-based approach. Before they begin their journey, do we welcome them with a discussion of the ideas of the day? Stories of inspiration and success? No. A young student, having arrived on campus, is immediately met by a series of messages warning about the dangers of being a university student. Sexual predators, disease, cheating, procrastination, academic and non-academic misconduct … the list is too long to recount here.

Once inside the classroom, we pass out binding contracts that describe course content, regulations, and grading schemes. Extra attention is given to the ways in which you can fail a course. Often these lists prohibit computers and smartphones in what can only be seen as a reminder that our universities are often preparing students for a wonderful life in the previous century. Student-run events promote themselves as a means to escape the suffering of classes, with the apex being the "spring break," when students have the chance to leave town and anesthetize themselves in order to escape the pain of university education. Frustrated professors remind students they should be happy to be there because there are people in other, poorer countries who would kill to take their place. Is this the best we can do? Is the peak of what we can offer something that is only good relative to torment and poverty?

A creative campus should begin with the assumption that most people are positive, dynamic individuals who want the best for themselves and others. Yes, there will be some bad behaviour from a few people at the university, but they are a tiny minority and can for the most part be avoided with simple precautions. A campus that is founded on trust will do a better job of inhibiting bad behaviour than one that seeks to terrify students with over-the-top descriptions of universities as places of moral depravity where you must always be on guard. Let us challenge one another to do better instead of warning ourselves of the worst.

The university should be a place where minds are nurtured and celebrated, not threatened and pitted against one another. So many issues are facing the world today that require us to engage fully that we must move past the state of fear and violence that grips most of our campuses. Every university has both universal and local concerns. All of us should be engaged in the issues that are confronting our world – globalization, IT, economic challenges, war, the arts, scientific discovery, the climate, poverty, and so on. In our own neighbourhoods, some issues will be of particular importance owing to local realities. For a change, let us focus on what actually matters.

We should make clear to students that we need them to engage at school so that they can build the world of tomorrow. Far too often, students are warned that they had better study hard or our uncertain world will punish them. Students are further cajoled into moving quickly through school in order to get into the workforce as quickly as possible. But the world has always been uncertain and always will be, so there is no rush to get out there and begin a job for which you have no calling. If instead we speak to students and welcome them to the life of ideas – to the stewardship of society – then we can enlist their help in tackling issues that matter. We need them to help, and it is in their interest to do so.

Students, staff, and faculty working together can become the engine for the Information Age. Let careers take care of themselves – forget about graduating as quickly as possible. A student who has a track record of discovery and working creatively in groups will have no problem securing employment. There is no rush to finish – we live longer and do more than ever before. We should encourage students to take the time to care for themselves, to find the work that calls to them and that will allow them to make the greatest contribution they can to society.

In our world there are wars, there is disease, and there is poverty. We have hundreds of thousands of critical essays on these topics. How many more do we need? Perhaps a lot, but how many? And how many creative approaches do we need? How many new ways of looking at these issues? Young students are the perfect people to turn their attention to these challenges. Before they have become steeped in the same thinking as those who created the problems, perhaps they could come up with useful suggestions.

These students have the greatest untapped resource on earth – invention, creativity, and love. Why should we train these people to treat every idea as suspect? To compete with one another? As Robinson says, we are born with love, but we *learn* to fear.[10]

If we want to compete, why not get serious about our opposition? Let us compete against cancer, against pollution, against civil war, against domestic violence, against poverty. Fight those foes and you can be a proud competitor – anything less and I am afraid you are letting us all down, and we just do not have any more time to spend on self-aggrandizing intellectualism. Socrates called it sophistry. Long, rhetorical battles merely for the sake of another article or book expend too much fuel for too little return. The practice is environmentally unsound.

Students like each other – they have a lot in common. The new university needs to find ways to keep them in the same room more often. We do not need to teach them to work together – they already know how to do that – we just need to stop separating them. A certain percentage of every degree should be focused on productive communication between groups. Engineers, artists, chemists, and computer scientists all need to benefit from networked communication in real time and space.

Teams of students from across the university need to take up project-based learning, such as programs for innovation in agriculture, transportation, or health care. The promise of young minds developing different specialties while working together is the single greatest hope for our planet. There is an old saying that the definition of insanity is to continue to do the same thing and expect a new result. We have been trying the same thing on university campuses for hundreds of years with the same results, yet we fight tooth and nail to continue doing what we have always done.

Donald Hall writes about the inherent violence of nostalgia on university campuses.[11] With change everywhere in society, we must free ourselves from the shackles of past practice and move on to the next age of being. The argument that we have "always done something this way," or "we used to do such and such," should be seen as a direct threat to ideas, creativity, and loving communication. That which was done in the past is – almost by definition – something we should question because *now* is no longer the past. Following Darwin, it is not the strongest or the smartest who survive – it is those who can adapt.[12] Once we decide to support adaptation, we find that opponents of change threaten the very life of ideas.

Why do students view university as something they *have* to do rather than something they *want* to do? We all started with a love of learning, of exploration and discovery, but at some point we became jaded. I suggest we take a long, hard look at what calms our intellectual waters. We often blame governments, administrators, and students, but I think it is time for us to take this on ourselves. We can all recall a time when we seemed to transform from beings that were driven to pursue the next idea to professionals whose lives are portioned out between meetings, marking, and a shrinking amount of time for what we really loved doing in the first place.

Academic meetings should be bristling with ideas. They should be crackling with excitement. Instead, we treat meetings with colleagues like prison sentences. Donald Hall points out that there is an inherently corrosive force behind this trend. Do you know anyone who likes academic meetings? Every one of us has colleagues who post cartoons about how bad academic meetings are on the doors to their offices. It would mark you out for ridicule to admit you enjoy meetings. But surely we must ask – when did we decide to accept this state of affairs? Those who refuse to embrace collegiality should be invited to leave the collegium at their earliest possible convenience.

The problem started when we decided that our meetings would be run as episodes of urban warfare. We all have countless stories of internecine conflict in departments – stories we share as part cautionary tales, part titillating adventure stories. Copies of *Robert's Rules of Order* are kept close at hand so that we can force civility on those with whom we should be closest in mind, method, and vision. When did we stop thinking of these events as meetings of the mind and start seeing them as zones of conflict? Critical thinking is at the heart of this animosity before the fact. As prefects of the suspicious mind, we enter each room ready to disagree, to take issue, to stake our claims to the truth. The result is that we waste thousands of hours each year fighting with one another when we should be banding together to find new ways to approach the issues of the day.

But let us go further back, to the source of our critical selves. To emerge as defenders of the faith, we first had to be defenders of our doctoral research. There is a reason why we call our final test in graduate school a defence. The Ph.D. is structured as one long test that converts even the most idealistic of young scholars into hardened warriors who can take on attacks from all comers. The way university degrees are structured reflects a deep commitment to a critical view of the world. Students first must pass a series of courses that are deemed essential to the discipline. They must then absorb long lists of texts, which they evaluate, categorize, and prepare for exhalation in the form of tests called comprehensives, candidacies, or some other such thing. By the time they are finally ready to do research and write their thesis or theses, their disciplinary identity has been fixed and they have demonstrated – with proof – that they have read the books they are supposed to read and hold the ideas they are supposed to hold. Successful completion of these tasks even comes with a quasi-identity – we are said to be ABD, or "all but dissertation."

Many students abandon their studies at the ABD point. The reasons vary, but most often they split into three categories: (1) I now hate the discipline and I am leaving to get real work; (2) I have run out of funding and I am leaving to get real work; or (3) both. Students who leave school at this point are seen as failures by their colleagues, by their supervisors, and most importantly by administrators, who know that the institution receives its funding partly based on completion rates. Of course, the real failure comes in what we do not say: perhaps they are the smart ones. They knew when to say "enough is enough, I will no longer allow myself to be treated this way."

The dissertation is a massive project that mixes original research with concessions to the members of the supervisory committee. The admonition that "it is a degree requirement, not your magnum opus," has saved many candidates from crossing over into full-blown madness. Before it is approved, the candidate must survive the "defence," during which a panel of experts – and often a public audience – interrogate the work. Examiners are provided with a copy of the dissertation well in advance so that they can show up with a list of comments and queries. All of which means that candidates must prepare themselves to be attacked. Afterwards, they must thank their attackers and hope they will be judged worthy of a passing grade. Here again, strict rules are in place to ensure fairness, given that the model itself does not promote it. (Those who wish to do anything with their dissertation once it is done will have to completely rework it, following guidelines to be found in a number of books that tell you how to convert one of them into something actually useful.)

No wonder we arrive on campus to become professional researchers and teachers with a defensive and possibly even aggressive approach to the world of ideas. Pity the poor student who happens to ask the professor a question that is somehow connected to an area of their work that came in for heavy scrutiny during the defence. The eyes of the instructor are sure to glass over as the sage on the stage assumes a defensive posture and launches tactic 172 in response to the logical fallacy gambit 147A.

More than a decade ago, Camille Paglia complained about the "Protestant high seriousness" that plagues university campuses.[13] Indeed, the stereotype of the successful academic – heartily lampooned by David Lodge, Kingsley Amis, and many others – is of an agonized mind trapped inside a neglected body wandering around campus weighed down by the sheer magnitude of their knowledge.[14] Everyone is their enemy – the government of the day does not appreciate them, the administration is out to get them, and the students are too dim to understand them. I agree with Paglia, but again I look farther back and deeper into the problem. It is true that some developments in the academy have suffered because of the type of stiff-upper-lip, antisocial trends in the Protestant line so strongly ossified by the American system that now dominates the world, but the Catholics before and after them suffered from an equally grim commitment to self-reproach. Still further back, the pagans before them both were beaten into a narrow vision of what it meant to be a citizen committed to thought. Right versus wrong has always been and always will be an intellectual tradition deeply connected to revenge narratives, and it started at the dawn of Western civilization.

Allow me to share an example. I am sure you will be able to supply your own. One of the first major conferences I attended was a meeting of the Modern Language Association (MLA). It is one of the largest academic meetings each year, and it is known for a few things. First, for years it was timed so that it fell over the Christmas holidays so that academics could avoid any social interaction with family and friends and stay focused on important issues related to their work. Second, it is a job fair for up-and-coming academics, most of whom will never find full-time work in the academy. Everyone in the discipline knows this, and there are countless essays reflecting on it. Regular features of the conference are candidates crying in elevators and washrooms full of vomiting job prospects succumbing to nerves. Third, the program for the conference is available to the public in advance, and without fail the local press publishes an article poking fun at the ridiculous titles of papers being presented. One or two of the organizers then write condescending responses to the journalists, who are assumed incapable of understanding our work. All are read out in the meetings of the MLA, and the tight-jawed critical class sneers at the plebian response to their work. Occasionally they emit an almost-laugh.

On my first trip to the MLA – and let me state at the outset that I have had some of the best experiences of my academic life at the yearly conference – I went to the opening address by the president. Each year, the president of the day shows charts that illustrate that the humanities are in crisis and that funding is being cut everywhere. The organization is well staffed, so they have data going back to the beginning of the society. The speakers assure the crowd they are doing everything they can to fight for the disciplines in the face of ever more threatening storms on the horizon.

From my very first time sitting in that room, I could not help but ask – if everything has been getting worse since the MLA was formed, why not disband it and try something else? I stand by that question and would now like to suggest that we consider disbanding most specialist organizations as one way of more fully integrating with our colleagues. I am glad to meet with people who are researching and teaching at the other end of the earth, but perhaps I should be spending a little more quality time with the scientist on the other side of the quad if I really want to be an engaged academic citizen. Just think of the jet fuel we would save and the relationships we would build that could help strengthen university governance. Rather than developing strong bonds with people who cannot help us in our programs, why not join our colleagues and build a stronger campus network?

Following this assertion, I would also like to ask, What if the newspaper reporters are right when they say our paper titles make no sense? What if we *are* writing about silly, meaningless things? What if we need to take the hint and maybe have a bit of a laugh at ourselves and get back to working on something that people actually care about reading and/or hearing?

Imagine if the reporters wrote about all of the compelling new ideas that scholars had come up with recently. What if, instead of having meetings with graphs about how everything is getting worse, we talked about how wonderful it is to teach and research and started sharing the best of ourselves with the outside world? My guess is that our enrolment numbers would start rising again and that we would not have to make up excuses for our ridiculous essay titles.

I do not want to leave the MLA before pointing to a positive example that I believe highlights a creative, open, and loving way of working. It also helps demonstrate that much is already happening to improve the academy. I would like to draw attention to the role Stephen Greenblatt has played in the study of modern languages.[15] For those outside this world of study it is hard to convey the importance of this one person in the world in which I began my academic work. Greenblatt has been the editor of major anthologies for his discipline and has authored several groundbreaking works with substantial public appeal. He even worked on the award-winning film *Shakespeare in Love*. While serving as president of the MLA, he wrote a powerful critique of the discipline's continued attachment to old models of publishing and evaluation and advocated for more open, dynamic models. He is also a staunch supporter of clear, jargon-free writing that is accessible to a wide audience.

My work as a student and then professional in his area coincided with the period of his greatest productivity, and I must say it has been a privilege. For years, I could not understand why his influence was so great, but I now believe I do. Back when I was a graduate student, everyone was reading and attacking his work. We were jealous, and it showed. How could someone achieve so much and always seem so happy? This was at a time when we were all giving up our love of English literature for its professional, critical implementation. I now realize that we resented his joy at a time when we were being taught to be professionally morose.

Over the years, Greenblatt has continued to publish exciting work and to attract readers on *and* off campus, and it occurs to me that I finally understand what he is doing. He is a hospitable author. He invites readers in and treats them like equals. He has, without a doubt, one of the most exciting minds working today, but you feel as though you are every bit his equal while in his company. In this way, he is an example of the future of scholarship: meticulous research generously shared.

But enough of literature – let us talk about the whole academic family.

Every year, we hear calls to increase interdisciplinary work and to expand the reach of our research. I would like to suggest that the solution to this lies at home and not out on the conference trail or in the pages of specialized journals. Once universities start to incentivize interaction on campus, they will begin to realize the potential that that can be unleashed when different minds are brought together.

Late in 2007, the Carnegie Mellon professor Randy Pausch gave his famous "Last Lecture."[16] He was young and had been diagnosed with inoperable cancer. His lectures had long been famous on campus, and they were about to become famous around the world. Pausch talked about a lot of things that day, but one thing that stood out for academics was his discussion of the institution where he worked. Carnegie-Mellon had made it possible for him to conduct completely open-ended, interdisciplinary work; indeed, the university had actively supported it. The results drew students and produced internationally recognized research. Pausch was infused with joy as he spoke about the work, his colleagues, the university's administrators, and his students.

There are a number of important messages in Pausch's last lecture. For us, the most important is that innovative, creative, and internationally important work begins at home. Let us stop spending so much on plane tickets and start spending money on creative spaces that bring us together to work, play, and learn at home. The only reason for universities to exist as discrete entities is to create an environment of exploration that benefits from the fact that everyone is together at the same time and in the same place. If this is not the case, we should convert our campuses into zones where only one discipline is pursued. You can move to the city where your colleagues are, and we can save money on jet fuel, cheap wine, bad cheese, and lanyards.

Richard Florida has created a vision of the world as run by the creative class. For him, "creatives" come from all disciplines but share one thing in common – they are creating rather than reproducing or repeating.[17] If we are to move toward a creative world, we need to check in with Florida. As the most recognized specialist in creativity, he is responsible for massive change around the world in both theoretical and practical terms. As a thinker, his books have influenced millions; whole cities and regions have been refashioned following his ideas and advice. Florida believes that the world belongs to creatives, but he is not very confident about what the university is doing to support them. How can this be? Are we not the engine of ideas? Do we not house centres of innovation? Host conferences on the imagination and entrepreneurship?

Like Florida, Daniel Pink can claim millions of devotees and demonstrate that vast regions of the earth have been changed by his work.[18] Pink shares Florida's lack of confidence in the university. Indeed, it is hard to find a creativity expert anywhere who does not see the university as actually hostile to creative work. A number of years ago, when I crossed the campus from the Department of English to that of Drama, I began reading these two scholars and their colleagues as part of a project that saw me heading up a program to design, implement, and teach a series of new courses that would serve the whole university. During my work, I made a very serious discovery about creativity: its enemy is not the university, but critical thinking.

Allow me to explain that initial discovery.

When you study all of the thinkers working on creativity, they tend to agree on its definition. I began this book with a version of that definition: to be creative you must "create something new that has value." Of course the challenge comes when we try to define *newness* and *value* and when we ask who might arbitrate such decisions. For our purposes, I hope we can agree that almost anything we accept as new owes its existence to pre-existing works or ideas – that is, we are not talking about *ex nihilo* creation. Value may be great or small and should not be thought of in monetary terms, but more along the lines of weight in the universe. Thus, if I come up with a new device that makes it easier for an arthritic patient to tie his shoelaces, I have created something new that has value. If I cure that person's arthritis, we can say the value is of greater weight. Value may be local and have greater or lesser mass.

When we think of creating things that are new and have value, we should keep as broad a view as possible. A new dance that an artist creates in order to explore a personal research interest can have value that is more difficult for us to appreciate from the outside than an invention we can hold in our hands. When that dancer later teaches students, choreographs a new piece, or performs in a production in a manner that builds from her work, we may see the results of her work more clearly, but the real newness and value were in the original exploration – it is just that it is easier for a layperson to see the expression in its more public form. We need to be aware that value is not greater when it is easier to see. At the heart of the university should always be the realization that pure research is both the greatest source of new ideas and the most inaccessible to easy evaluation. That is why researchers making those breakthroughs need tenure.

But we run into a problem when we try to reconcile critical thinking with creative work. The simple reason is that with critical thinking, merely rejecting something is sufficient to complete one's task. Critical thinking only requires us to take in information, question its assumptions, and break it into segments. There is no requirement for newness or value in critical work unless we grant that criticism is valuable in itself. Some do take this position, but even these individuals would be hard pressed to demonstrate a value for this work outside those circles that create critical work and then tell us it is valuable. There is no outside market for most criticism. It is a closed loop. Those who make the most money from its production are also its greatest proponents. Not much of a surprise there!

At the risk of oversimplifying, the newness feature in criticism sometimes amounts to little more than new ways to reject things that have already been rejected. There is no compunction to make a contribution or introduce an innovation in the area being scrutinized. Indeed, if there were a solution, the critic would be out of work. This nihilistic approach to knowledge runs counter to a creative approach, which takes in information and, rather than attacking it, offers new information inspired by that engagement.

The one true exception to this is genuine dissent. The tradition of recording dissenting positions is an important one. Still, even here we might begin to ask – would we not benefit from a system that recorded a series of views rather than one decisive position and one dissenting? What do we sacrifice in order to ensure that our decision-making procedures fit within a yes/no, right/wrong mode?

Bearing the mark of its history, critical thinking's most dangerous component may well be its propensity for convincing us we should accept less. We can find ourselves overwhelmed by its infinite stream of complaint. Hopelessly outmatched by the problems of the world, we give up and lose the capacity to act. Creativity, by contrast, always asserts that we *can* do something. This is why critical thinking is inherently repressive and ultra-conservative in the sense that it continually positions itself in opposition to action, creation, and engagement. It is reactionary to the core.

For the creative mind, when something comes its way the response is "yes, and ..." The creative mind welcomes communication and attempts to respond in kind. It is an open, loving way of engaging with others that begins by extending the original speaker, writer, or communicator the benefit of the doubt. The other has taken the trouble to speak; therefore I will go to the trouble of listening and responding.

The critical act begins before anyone speaks. We assume a posture of suspicion and remain vigilant lest someone say something we disagree with – which of course is everything to one degree or another. Once a statement is made, it is separated into its component parts, evaluated, and then attacked on points of content for one or more of its segments or on the merits of its connective tissues, or both. It treats others as suspect before they even engage; in this way it creates an environment of hostility before we even begin to communicate.

When I began to question the merits of critical thinking I was often accused of not understanding what critical thinking is – a point I am more than willing to concede. I was trained in critical thinking and did design and teach advanced university courses in criticism and critical theory, but I am willing to accept that I could be mistaken or that I am somehow deceived, perhaps even delusional. But of one thing I am certain: people who produce nothing but critical thinking make the only statements I can find that say we need more critical thinking in the world. We do not have governments, companies, or schools asking for an increase in the supply of it. For me the reason is clear: the market is glutted. You can decide for yourself.

As a result of the overproduction of criticism, markets for ideas are emerging on the edges of universities. Specialists in education, performance, and creative thinking are collaborating with artists, engineers, politicians, and activists off campus. Long ago, Christopher Marlowe had to leave the university in order to produce his best work; Shakespeare later outdid him by rejecting the academy entirely; today we are again heading toward a creative explosion supported by a revolution in IT. They had print; we have digital. Their revolution was large and moved quickly; ours is massive and is moving at lightning speed.

As with the first Incunabular period when we moved from manuscript to print technology, those with a stake in the past accuse anyone involved in innovation of threatening the very fabric of society. Their fear is completely understandable. Change is unsettling, all the more so when it causes such large shifts in such a short time.

There is no question whatsoever that the university students I teach today are fundamentally different from those I studied with in the 1990s. We are not talking about the traditional shift from generation to generation; rather, this is a seismic occurrence the likes of which occur only once or twice in a millennium. There is also no question that much about the university has remained unchanged in the face of this transformation. Those whose identities are deeply connected to the older world cannot help but be frightened that they are living through such an evolution. Their way of being is vanishing.

For this brief period of time – from now until our generation of academics passes through the working world – there will exist a deep tension between the younger cohort's inherent knowledge of new technology and our lack of shared experience in the area. As faculty, we are light years behind our students in this area, and many of us can expect to remain so for our entire careers (of course there are exceptions). But we have no need to apologize for the fact that we are the last generation of the print age. We had a good run, but it is over. The only way we can be guilty of a dereliction of duty is if we fail to acknowledge our ignorance and take steps to remain current. Fortunately, there is a ready-made way to move forward. If we embrace creativity, we will increase our ability to adapt, and adaptation is the key to the future.

The university must become a place that supports the Information Revolution in the ways it is best suited to do so. The academy has always staked a claim on information and positioned itself as the keeper of data. To get a charter as a university, an institution has to demonstrate that it has a sufficient library with adequate holdings in all the requisite areas. As we move away from hard copies of work and as libraries begin to warehouse older books at remote locations, we must not get hung up thinking that we are losing the best of what we do. Instead we should remember that it was always an academic's expertise at guiding others through information that was required. The Information Age needs the academy to become expert guides to the future. This means a creative engagement with information and a positive, proactive approach to change.

Some may argue that one way to serve the Information Age is to sharpen our critical tools to stem the streams of data, but there is simply too much information coming at us. It is no longer possible to pretend we live in an analogue world. More importantly, there is essential work to address our transformation that can only be done by the academy, and that work needs to be done now. The academic's job is to remain current and work to serve society. A failure to remain current today would leave our fellow citizens unsupported in the time of the greatest change in history. It would amount to a profound betrayal of our responsibilities to scholarship.

The university at its best has always fought for the freedom of ideas and their dissemination. We are currently experiencing extraordinary change in the way that information moves between individuals and institutions. Parties who have an interest in controlling data are working hard to shut down access, to control information sharing, and to seed the Internet with messages they have an interest in promoting. Academics need to advocate for an open, hospitable, and loving world of information. Those who have tenure have an obligation to use it for what it was designed for – to protect freedom of inquiry, freedom of speech, and the rights of all people to access their culture.

Scholars such as Michael Geist and Lawrence Lessig are pioneers of the new academic world.[19] As powerful as the numbers of Internet users are, they need the support of the academy in making the case for shared access to information. A creative world can only exist if access to information is unfettered. Just as Shakespeare was able to thrive during a time of unprecedented access to information, unregulated language, and loose rules regarding intellectual property, so we can only benefit from the new technological revolution if we keep information free and if we do not treat ideas as if they were things to be bought and sold.

If critical thinkers with great skills in attacking arguments wish to join the creative fight, they should stop fighting with other academics and join the discussion over intellectual property, IT, and open access. These issues are connected to the very core mission of universities, and the conversation would benefit from more voices.

Just as people born before the Information Revolution now run universities, so lawmakers are from the last generation raised on critical thinking and print technology. Various groups are working hard to find the best way to operate in a global information climate, and we need to have productive discussions about the universal benefits to be had from open access. Those conversations will fundamentally challenge much of property law and require consideration by informed jurists.

In some ways the argument is as old as society itself. Plato argued that we must control people's access to information if we wish to have them serve in the roles for which we deem them to be best suited. Some of us do not believe this is the best path. Some of us believe that Plato's position was tainted by his anger at a society that took away his beloved master. When we look at the history of our world since that time, every regime that has sought to control information to its people has been guilty of greater violence than those that allowed open access.

Writers like Christopher Hitchens have argued that religion is responsible for most of the world's problems. I would argue that it is not religion that is dangerous – it is organizations that wish to take control of information. Those who argued with Hitchens – all of whom he more than vanquished when he addressed them in public – pointed out that movements like Stalinism and Nazism were not religious. He stretched his definition to show that these institutions were built on religion, but it is an easier route to point out that any organization that seeks to control information is in danger of becoming tyrannical. All totalitarian regimes fit this description.

The university and our colleagues in the media have in their shining moments stood for free inquiry. To do so now would be to engage in a wonderfully creative act – it would certainly support new ideas that have value and would serve the best of the historical mission of the academy.

Our academic meetings should be discussions of freedom and exploration, our research should be bold, new, and ever expanding, and our teaching should reflect the fact that while we may be experts in some areas we are all turning fresh faces toward the twenty-first century. We all have a lot to learn. If we can do this – if we can foster centres of creativity – we can save ourselves the worry of being irrelevant, of finding students who still want to learn, and of maintaining the long history of the professoriate. This age requires a creative response, and it will move rapidly past us if we do not answer the call, but it will carry us like no other force yet encountered if we embrace the best parts of ourselves and move into the future together.

Chapter 6

"Sure, It Works in Practice, but Will It Work in Theory?"

There is an old joke on university campuses that has two figures speaking while looking at some form of academic product. As the work is successfully demonstrated in front of them, the more serious of the two figures turns to the other and says, "Sure, it works in practice, but will it work in theory?"

If we want to change the way society works, we should start with universities. Universities are the engines of ideas in our society. They are the places where we train our kindergarten and high school teachers, our religious and political leaders, our executives, scientists, artists, and academics. They are the realms of the modern-day version of Plato's philosopher kings. Not everyone needs to or should go to university, but universities, when they are working properly, should help us all.

On the university campus there are three separate areas of research and teaching that then break down into many smaller units. The basic areas are Arts, Sciences, and Professional Schools. When universities were first developed they followed a model usually referred to as the liberal arts. Liberal in this compound means liberating, so these studies were the studies meant to free the individual from the bonds of ignorance. The liberal arts were paired with the servile arts – as in "service to one's fellow citizens" – the study of which was meant to help us achieve our highest potential.[1] This formula was designed so that first we would free ourselves, and then, in light of our particular talents, we would turn to our role as citizens. These models have been recast a number of times, but you can still see that the old liberal arts are represented in the arts and sciences (with the social science disciplines combining the two). This type of education does not necessarily lead to a profession that has the same name as the degree. Thus, a philosophy major may not end up with a job called "philosopher" but will instead use his or her educated mind to serve society in a role that makes the best use of that particular person's gifts. Or at least that is the idea. The highest goal in this tradition was to use one's talents to the best of one's abilities in service of one's fellow citizens. Laudable stuff.

I used to work in the liberal arts, but I now spend more of my time in the servile arts. The servile arts (those that are designed to immediately serve our fellow citizens) are what we now think of as the professional faculties – nursing, medicine, education, the performing arts, law, and engineering. The early idea of education was that the best path to the servile arts was to study the liberal arts first and then progress to the next level, but as education has grown increasingly specialized, this combination has been mostly abandoned. The result has been an increasingly fragmented campus that many wish to reintegrate. Different periods have different names for it, but currently the term *silos* is what we hear on campuses and in boardrooms. In this model, we all go to the campus, exist in our particular silos, and have no contact with anyone else on campus.

Before we go any further, we need to take a moment to reflect on the servile arts. In the run-up to the publication of this book, I was fortunate enough to receive feedback from two groups of peer reviewers. In both cases, a reader was upset by my use of the term servile, as if it were a pejorative. What a telling reaction. For the ancient Greeks, to be of service to others was the highest calling to which one could aspire. What does it mean that today, to be of service is seen as a negative? Perhaps the solitary position of the critical thinker as the person who must stand apart deflating ideas is caught up in this evaluation. The liberated thinker remains ever on guard celebrating the triumph of the individual to remain free. What might it mean for our universities if we are interested only in personal freedom and not in service to our colleagues, our students, and the broader society? The answer to this question deserves its own book, but we should pause for a moment to observe the strong reaction that has settled around the notion of service. Following the Classical model, if we were only to spend our time devoted to the liberal arts, and never take up service, we would – by definition – be entirely selfish. Here again I believe our current model has left us separated from ourselves.

The observation many people make these days is that our students suffer from a lack of interaction with their fellow learners in other disciplines. Surveys such as the National Survey of Student Engagement (NSSE) indicate that students share these concerns. On campus, colleagues from different areas continually speak about the difficulty of interacting with other academics. Both researchers and societal stakeholders have united in a call for greater integration in order to address the challenges of the twenty-first century.

The change I am proposing would address these issues. For that change to work, we need to address three areas on the university site: the content of courses, their means of delivery, and the mission of the university campus as a whole. In this chapter, we look at how we might do this.

Students leave campus to enter a workforce (and in this category I include academic work) that is increasingly seeking dynamic individuals who can work in a variety of ways. As we discover new ways to use technology to replace any repeatable task – including the delivery of prefabricated lectures – we are finding that human beings are only needed for engaged, dynamic work that taps into their creative potential and their ability to get along with others in the moment.

Let us look at one way that a university campus could move away from the critical and toward the creative:

When we look at the problem of silos on campus, we find that the easiest ways to achieve reintegration are through service courses. Courses that appeal to all students on campus and are offered as options can become meeting places for twenty-first-century students. Implementing these courses is easy, cheap, and popular with students. The biggest challenge is staffing these classes, and here again there is a simple solution: instead of merely hiring sessionals from a single discipline, the courses should be taught by interdisciplinary scholars or carved up and team-taught.

For these courses to work, faculty members need to be willing to allow these offerings to be marked in a generous fashion. If we are to invite engineers, economists, and English majors to take part in a creativity course, we need to find ways that will allow all of these students the comfort to select these offerings without the risk of tanking their GPA and losing their scholarship or their ability to continue in their major. The competitive nature of critical thinking continues in our grading systems, but these obstacles are too large to address campus-wide – instead, let us create pass/fail or easily accessible versions of courses that everyone can take as a first step. Our obsession with grade ranking will take care of itself once we move away from a hostile approach to education.

These courses should focus on aspects of creative thinking that are relevant to all students. Courses that focus on creativity, the fine arts, story, performance, memory, love and happiness, and other such broad-spectrum topics with connections to the world of creative work allow everyone to engage with issues that matter to us all. A foundational principle of creative work is that we must be willing to take risks and we must be willing to fail. Failing in our exploration of ideas should not be met with a mark on a transcript that will follow us for the rest of our lives. We must allow students to explore and experiment and reward them when they take chances rather than when they perfectly replicate skills related to areas they are already strong in. No one is interested in a student who has become a perfect answer-giving machine. Computers do that better than we do, so that type of education is a losing proposition.

If you are going to offer these courses, you need to give up on strict grading regimens. The goal is to engage students from all departments, and the only way to do that is to find a way that makes success possible for a wide variety of students. After years of being conditioned to work only for marks, students will need support in order to experiment with a more open form. The model and the content will be new, so educators need to assure students that they are not going to harm their academic profiles by taking these course offerings.

It is easier to conduct these types of courses as options or service courses rather than something else. Grading systems that involve pass/fail or more generous marking schemes are necessary to ensure success. Some will argue that we should compel all students to engage in these classes in the same way we currently compel them to become critical thinkers, but as a first step it will be easier to focus only on option courses and let students self-select. My experience is that this will draw students from all sectors of the university. It is also easier for our more reluctant colleagues to accept.

To reach students, professors and administrators need to work with student advisers. Advisers are on the front lines of course selection, and they will be able to help you groom your course offerings to address the needs of your student body. Later, they will be able to share information about your creative classes with students on campus. If your project fails, it was only a few option courses; if it succeeds, you can propose expanding the offerings.

With relatively few courses, you can expose every student on campus to the creative approach to work. They will still face critical thinking in most classes, but questions will arise from these small offerings and chances are they will spread. These lower-level classes will only begin the dialogue on campus. At some point, students will want higher-level offerings that focus on smaller, creative units working toward common goals. These projects will almost necessarily be offered by interdisciplinary scholars or team-taught by interested groups. At the higher level, supervisory work should replace more traditional lecture and seminar forms. There is also the potential for distance collaboration using multimedia and various networking models.

Closely connected to these upper-level classes will be faculty research. Funding agencies are increasingly asking faculty to find ways to include undergraduate students and greater numbers of graduate students in cutting-edge research. There is no reason why upper-level creative courses could not be linked directly to research programs or small portions of larger projects. Students would benefit from work in pure research, and faculty would be provided with small teams that can help them with ongoing programs of academic and professional inquiry. The creation of something new that has value sounds an awful lot like research to me!

One of the largest challenges will occur when we try to find ways to grade the work of students in creative programs. If we are to incentivize risk, failure, and valiant attempts that teach but go nowhere, we will need to leave a great deal of leeway in the hands of professors, who will have to find new ways to provide grades for student work. It is certainly the case that critical thinking models fit well with numerical grading systems, but it is too simple to say that we can go without evaluation as we move toward a more creative form of education. The way in which student work is evaluated must be given serious consideration, as reports are often the chief means of streaming students into areas of expertise as they move forward in their working lives. If a student is not well suited to working in one area, giving them a false positive does not help their long-term creative potential. Genuine feedback is essential. Competency-based protocols are popular in some areas but would require work to serve all areas of the academy.

In larger classes where we focus on creative content, we will be able to support student exploration in only a few ways. It is difficult to have two-hundred-plus students doing multimedia projects or other such work. In large service classes, students should be introduced to the ways in which creative work can be applied to their own disciplines. To that end, it is important to expose them to key creative thinkers as well as to creative content. Most creativity courses include some content from the fine arts (art, dance, drama, and music), but we should not limit ourselves to traditional arts. Explorations in multimedia, in engineering, in creative business models, and in scientific experimentation could all be part of the content. Group projects can be of great use in larger sections and can simplify marking.

With group projects, some students will hide behind others' work and merely collect the credit or a grade – this is unavoidable. However, attempts to clamp down on these students will not give us the results we desire. Creative classes cannot resort to draconian models simply so that we can capture the small number of students who are padding their records with a class they do not take seriously. In my own experience, the percentage of students who abuse more open formats is very small. By the time students arrive in a creative course they are so excited to be able to work in an open way with their fellow students that most of them do much more work than is required. I would speculate that the energy of highly motivated students convinces the less engaged ones to become involved. Early classes focusing on creativity were implemented to enrich the educational experience of students whose programs did not include any work in traditionally creative areas; however, if we wish to develop truly creative programs, we need to leave these models behind and recognize that creativity is not housed in any one discipline. If we are not supporting risk and experimentation in the traditional fine arts, then faculty, staff, and students in those areas need as much support as anyone else to reconnect with creative ways of working. Just because you work in the arts does not mean you are creative.

Of course, the fine arts – particularly in their newer, multidisciplinary forms – will remain at or near the centre of creative work. Where their contribution needs to grow is in the public discussion of creativity. A glance at the available works on the subject shows that social scientists and business people are writing most of the books in the field. Even medical researchers are involving themselves in the conversation to a greater degree. Scientists and artists need to join this discussion in such a way that their contributions can be understood by the general public and by our colleagues in different departments. The fine arts and pure sciences define themselves as disciplines committed to the discovery of new and valuable things, and a more robust discussion of creative practices would be welcome.

Key to the development of creative work is communication. Campuses need to provide the greatest possible exposure to working groups. If creativity means creating something new that has value, production should be easy to gauge, be it when marking students or evaluating faculty. To support campus-wide creativity, yearly evaluations should include a section for rewarding those who contribute to projects.

Deans, provosts, and other officers of the university need to be brought on board for any project that seeks fundamental change. In my experience, these individuals are often easier to convince than others because their work requires a commitment to interdisciplinarity and an awareness of change both within the university and outside it. These individuals can provide new means of supporting creative work. Academics have only so much time, and once they realize that creative work can help them advance in their field, they will allocate time to it. Most academics *want* to pursue their passion anyway – we just need to set them free.

Administrators also have a large role to play. Universities are complex bureaucracies, and an ability to streamline various protocols and paper trails is necessary to enhance creative work. One way to advance creative work is by cutting any bureaucratic red tape that is impeding the path to dynamic collaboration. Here again, senior administrators must incentivize all work that makes other work easier. Less paper, fewer forms, and more support for grant writing, the acquisition of space, and connections with investment sources could help ignite a creative revolution on campus. As Donald Hall points out, most administrators are dedicated individuals who just want to make their institutions better, and this is one way they could do so.

The simplest way to engage administrators and staff is by implementing a policy whereby anyone responsible for adding a layer of bureaucracy is given a demerit and anyone who implements a program that streamlines the university's work is given a bonus. Administrators are talented people and should be left to reimagine the university; but if they are to do so, we must support them in the same way they support us. Bureaucracies that are left on their own expand exponentially. If we hope to have a creative university, then we must provide our colleagues in administration with the tools to reach their full potential. Similarly, they should be rewarded for efficiency and given demerits for administrative glut.

Likewise, committee work should only count toward service requirements for faculty and staff when something is achieved. When a committee stagnates, or fails to carry out the task it was assigned, the work should not count toward work for that calendar year. This simple alteration would prioritize dynamic engagement and discourage stasis. Productive committees are more fruitful for the university and make better use of the members' time. Currently, we incentivize quantity rather than quality of academic service, which is entirely backward. Yet again, this approach meshes well with a critical mindset that treats every new idea and every colleague with great trepidation. If instead we helped academics understand that working together is easier and more beneficial, they would be happier in these pursuits.

Diversity supports creative work. Given that creativity feeds on ideas, the more information we have the better. When we have input from a wider pool of contributors, we improve the overall quality of creative experience. Traditionally, we have thought of this in terms of students from overseas or from other provinces, but we should also think in terms of age. With a large portion of the population getting set to retire, universities should vigorously recruit mature students. It was the baby boomers who expanded universities in the first place, and they are a highly motivated and highly educated bunch. The potential to be realized from a meeting of the minds between experienced professionals returning to school and new students is extraordinarily exciting. Also, retired professionals with pools of talent should be sought after for adjunct positions, because they have much to offer and do not face the financial pressure of having to support themselves through academic labour.

The academic community is already moving toward a more creative model. A quick review of the major granting agencies and the statements of university presidents and boards of governors shows a new commitment to innovation, invention, and creativity. On campus, these laudable goals must be met by introducing incentive packages that reward innovation and discourage stagnation. New and experimental work should count toward promotion; gridlock on committees and a failure to remain current should be discouraged and show up as a negative on evaluations. If we hope to move to more positive practices, we must actively discourage negative work on campus. When colleagues struggle with this, professional development options should be made available.

The world beyond the academy has already changed. That is why we are witnessing such a transformation in the student body. These changes are directly connected to the IT revolution and to demographics, but they are also a consequence of expanded access to education. The greater the pool of talent, the better off our institutions and in turn our societies will be, so we need to maintain a commitment to nurturing a diverse student population in order to create the richest possible field for the imagination.

We should now look at some further specifics. I want to share three examples of how we can enhance creativity on campus. By starting small we can test whether we want to go all the way and attempt to structure our institutions along creative rather than critical lines. The first case I will share is the project that started my work on this book. The second describes a model of work that lies behind that project. The third is a personal model for reigniting or nurturing the creative in your work. All three are easily transferable to any campus.

This book is the outgrowth of an experiment we have been conducting at the University of Calgary over the past several years. While not all of the work we have done will translate, I believe it provides a useful case study. The project began as a research endeavour, then expanded into a pedagogi-cal experiment and finally into a series of articles, interviews, and public speeches. The book you are reading arose from requests to follow up on this work in monograph form. The experiment will continue as I attempt to integrate what I have heard – and will hear – back.

In the academic year 2007–8, a working group of faculty members from the University of Calgary's Faculty of Fine Arts began to study student information and curriculum options. That group met for more than a year, analyzed data from international, national, and local surveys, and held a retreat in order to synthesize the information they had gathered. One of the group's final recommendations was that some new fine arts courses be created that would serve students from all faculties on campus.

The work this group conducted focused on the well-known National Survey of Student Engagement (NSSE) and various follow-up studies conducted on our campus. The committee determined there was a need for courses that brought a wide variety of students together to work in classes that contained creative content and that modelled creative ways of working together. The fine arts had traditionally functioned as a set of disciplines lodged between professional and arts programs. The terminal degree in this area is the Master of Fine Arts or MFA, which is often compared to the MBA or Master of Business Administration. The average age of an MFA student is much higher than for traditional master's students because the expectation in most programs is that students are returning to school after gaining experience as professional artists. This age difference again has parallels to the MBA, where ideally, students return to school with business experience before pursuing the degree.

As a result of clear signals from studies of students' needs and interests, and with an eye toward offering courses that would demonstrate the unique manner of work that the fine arts promote, we highlighted several subject areas for further research. These general areas of research and teaching were deemed to be of universal interest for students, while also carrying deep connections to the fine arts and its way of conducting research.

In the academic year 2008–9, I was hired to take the findings compiled by the group and to study them with an eye toward designing and piloting courses in two of the focal areas as a test of the research. The first two topic areas selected were creativity and story. These two subject areas were both of interest to university students and were intricately connected to the type of work conducted by researchers and professionals in the fine arts, but also in the professional world.

The classes drew students from every faculty on campus. The course outlines I presented included four short writing assignments of five hundred words each and one longer essay of two thousand words for each semester. There were also creative events that students had to attend, as well as mid-term and final exams. I set no upper limit for the writing projects and was happily surprised to find that given that freedom, the vast majority of students did much more work than was required. Indeed, most did more than double what they were asked. I invite you to draw your own conclusions about why. The classes were filled to capacity and had long waiting lists. As we developed more offerings, those too filled with long lists of students from every faculty seeking to enrol. This success continues today, more than five years into the project.

Once I began to study creativity more deeply it became apparent that there was a dearth of information in the field from working and/or teaching artists. This caused me concern and seemed to cry out for further study. If one goal of the original research committee was to promote the models of practice of the fine arts, then we would need to address this issue as part of our project.

The areas where work on creativity is currently the strongest are sports, education, business, and social science. Oddly, there is very little on the subject in the arts and fine arts disciplines. In general, sports, education, and business models study creativity as a function of performance. Studies show that we can enhance our academic and work potential by developing our creativity, and each of these areas has a mandate to pursue that development. Thus, each has a wide array of publications in print and other media available. An interesting correlation exists in the arts and humanities: an increasing emphasis on critical thinking has meant a decreased emphasis on overtly creative work.

The social sciences pursue creativity in a slightly different fashion than an artist might. Our colleagues in anthropology, for example, have an interest in culture that has produced a steady stream of work in the area. Perhaps most famously, author, scholar, and researcher Wade Davis has made cultural ecology a lifelong mission.[2] Davis was an early advocate of cultural diversity as a means for addressing the world's challenges. His books are engaging and accessible narratives. He understands the power of creativity.

Perhaps the best-known area of creativity studies focuses on economics. Richard Florida and Daniel Pink have sparked a huge amount of research into creativity, creative practice, and the movements and behaviours of creative and non-creative populations. Their work has links to philosophy, political science, and business, but the models they use are firmly rooted in the type of demographic and behavioural studies that belong to economics and business.

Both Florida and Pink have isolated an explosion in creativity in the world of work. Globalization and the recent technological revolution are converging in ways that are transforming world markets, modes of working, and all forms of communication. Florida and Pink, and a host of others, agree there will be winners and losers as a result. The losers will be those who fail to come to terms with the change and its magnitude. The winners will be those who create something *new* that *has value* – the "creatives." Governments, companies, and schools around the world are pushing projects that emphasize creativity and its power to improve all aspects of our lives. The key is adaptation.

Most of the experts in the area argue that the university is not doing a very good job at promoting this new work. But we should celebrate the fact that most of these researchers were trained at post-secondary institutions and that their research funding came through academic appointments. Many of them have had to move off campus to continue their work, but most – if not all – universities are now pursuing programs that will promote many of the initiatives supported by experts in creativity.

Artists have largely been missing from these discussions, with one important exception: those working in arts education were promoting these ideas before they came into vogue, and they continue to make valuable contributions. Many of them are working artists who support their practice with research and teaching careers. Most artists contribute to the work on creativity following one of two paths. First, they publish essays that protest the lack of funding or support for the arts in society in general and the academy in particular. These protestations are in many ways well founded, and those leading the charge hope to take advantage of the current climate of change. They hope to have funding renewed or to restore arts programs, and they use the increased demand for creative work as evidence that they should be supported. The challenge for these groups will be to prove that they are working creatively rather than merely repeating old practices – that they do not expect to benefit merely because they come from a field that has traditionally placed a higher premium on the creative. If we recall our definition of creativity as involving the creation of something new that has value, then those of us working in the creative and performing arts may face some tough questions. Are we truly being creative, or have we too become the prisoners of worn-out models of production?

Second, they attempt to share personal forms of artistic practice that readers can emulate. Books such as Julia Cameron's *The Artist's Way* and Michael J. Gelb's *How to Think Like Leonardo da Vinci* fall into this category. These books are certainly useful for some, but there remains a serious gap in terms of more directly targeted commentary on the role of creative practice in society and the ways this form of work might be pursued, promoted, or developed on campuses, at work, or in our personal lives.

Within the artistic community, two reasons are given for the lack of interest in publishing work on creative practice. The first is obvious: genuinely productive artists – who are the ones we wish to learn from – are too busy working as artists to stop and write about working as artists. The second issue is that many artists are committed to the idea that their particular method of artistic practice is so effective that they alone should train others in its protocols and that only those they approve of should replicate their work. The challenge here is that it does not allow for differences between individuals. This attitude can – and does – have its benefits, but it is an inherently conservative approach to creativity. There are widely divergent ways of working creatively, so we need to step back and look for shared practices and other points of interest that *can* be shared with a broader audience. Think of it this way – the best way to be like Leonardo da Vinci is to avoid reading books about *how* to be like him and instead just *be* him – what you need to learn is how to be the best version of yourself.

During my professional life I have had the very good fortune to work in the corporate world, the government, the academy, and a number of artistic circles. I have been a designer, a writer, a musician, and a theatre artist. In my time working with various groups and consulting with others, I have made a few observations that may be useful for our discussion.

The chief difference between a creative group and a critical one is that the former gets things done while the latter talks about things getting done. The easiest example here is a theatre group. I often think of my work on a production of Shakespeare's *A Midsummer Night's Dream* when I discuss the theatrical approach to work. The project I have in mind involved welders, carpenters, electricians, high school teachers, university teachers, students, actors, musicians, designers, costume and makeup professionals, choreographers, a fight director, a director, a textual consultant, and a voice expert.

What you notice immediately when working on a theatrical event is that an incredibly diverse group of people with very different backgrounds are working simultaneously. Also, theatre productions almost always function with tiny budgets and tight deadlines. All of us are familiar with the phrase "the show must go on," which gives name to the urgency of the work involved. Theatre people always get done on time and on budget. Or at least, they do so more often than anyone else I have ever encountered.

Steve Jobs famously said, "Real artists ship." To be creative means to actually produce something new that has value. A true artist – a true creative person – must *do* something. In the theatre, this has meant that hundreds of thousands of teams have come together with a goal in mind and have almost always done exactly what they set out to do. Why are they able to do so when so many government, business, and academic projects wander in the weeds? It is because theatre projects prioritize creative work, while others focus on the critical. Critical minds book more meetings, strike sub-committees, and argue over terms of reference. Theatre groups identify a goal, begin work, and achieve that goal – every single time.

Within the creative model there is a strong incentive to reach the goal that helps mitigate one of the deadliest forms of critical thinking – personal quarrels. All of us work with congenial people and with others who are not. We have all watched personal battles hamstring organizations that should have been focusing on more important issues. I do not believe there is any way to get to a place where everyone on a team will get along – in fact, some difference of opinion is natural and productive. But there are aspects of organizations that can render them prone to particularly destructive forms of combat.

Political scientist Wallace Sayre famously said that "academic politics is the most vicious and bitter form of politics, because the stakes are so low." We all know it, yet the problem persists. You will by now be able to predict that I am going to suggest that working under the flag of critical thinking is at the heart of the problem. How could it not be? We suspect one another, and have been trained in rhetorical combat, so we are destined to have battle after battle in long-drawn-out and nuanced ways. It is impossible to calculate, but I would imagine we waste tens of millions of dollars a year at universities on time committed to fighting these low- or no-stake battles. In some of these battles, junior faculty and graduate and undergraduate students are collateral damage, and careers are lost or permanently harmed.

If we incentivized productivity, useless quarrelling would end. Deadlines make this happen almost instantly. In the theatre we are known for heightened, even outrageous emotion. The result is that we often have huge outbursts during our work on a show. Given that we have to keep on schedule, however, these disagreements are dealt with immediately. They have to be, because we are all focused on the goal, which causes us to realize that we have to find a way to work together. If instead we let people stew in the chemical cocktail released into their bloodstreams by their fight-or-flight reflexes, nothing gets done and we begin to look like the average academic committee.

The same happens in the world of music. If you are fortunate enough to put a band together that can gel musically and get along over the long term – which is very rare – at some point you will get a performance or recording contract. At that point, a whole new set of interested parties enter your lives. If you can work together you will succeed, if you quarrel you will fail. Again, creativity rewards productivity and punishes combat.

In the corporate and government worlds, similar incentive packages motivate teams. If your team has a goal, if everyone has a job that is necessary, and if the group feels they are working for a reason, you will have productive collaboration for as long as it is required. If instead you have people who spend more time talking about work than doing it, your group will soon be at a standstill and office politics rather than office productivity will be its defining characteristic.

In *The Cost of Bad Behavior: How Incivility Is Damaging Your Business and What to Do about It,* Christine Pearson and Christine Porath reveal the results of several decades of research into the world of work both on and off campus.[3] The results are overwhelming. Critical people contribute less to your organization; indeed, they impede progress and can cause your group to fail. One point will serve as an example: their book points out how often negative influences in meetings are able to govern the day while the rest of us try not to make waves. The result is damaged relationships, wasted meetings, and frustrated colleagues. The worst, however, comes when the researchers explain the drive that bullies have to grow their influence. Bullies work as hard as they can to get on hiring committees in order to breed themselves. Critical thinking does all it can to take over our organizations and bleed them of any creative potential. Thankfully, with all of this new research we are finally coming to realize that loving, compassionate ways of working are far more powerful than command-and-control tactics from the past.

Let's do a thought experiment:

In your department, workplace, or relationships, do you know of someone who is constantly complaining about work? Do they seem to spend more time talking about how hard they work and how unfair their lives are than they do actually working? We all know people like that – they exist in all organizations. Now ask yourself, are they being creative? How would you describe their behaviour?

In a society that trains all of its students in critical thinking, we groom ourselves to accept incessant complaining as acceptable and even intelligent behaviour. But what if what complainers are doing, rather than witty, informed social commentary, is corrosive? What if it not only harms our ability to work but also damages the workplace as a whole? Pearson and Porath's research demonstrates that continual criticism actually harms all those who witness it. How would your workday change if these people in your organization felt integrated, productive, and committed to a meaningful goal?

Over the past few decades we have all been discussing ways to become more interdisciplinary, but serious challenges prevent us from making progress. When we recall that critical thinking is a mode of thought that resists change at all costs, we can see why this is a problem. Each of us has retreated into our own corner of the campus and put up walls around our discipline. Often we have done so because there are so few of us left that we feel as if we are the last soldiers defending a castle built by our forebears. Of course, that is because that is exactly what is happening. We are fighting to maintain disciplines that were made for another time – a time that needed factory workers and corporate drones. Who ever imagined that *we* would become the conservative enemies of ideas and that the outside world would be the realm of exploration?

Disciplines behave exactly as that word suggests. They are defined by rules, regulations, and codes of behaviour. To join a discipline, you first have to pass through an initiation. Once safely inside the discipline, group members police one another to ensure that the discipline's requirements are met. Acolytes with minimal status sign up for program minors, those who are more dedicated are majors, and those who qualify and who agree to submit to the strictest rules possible become honours students. The narrower your focus, the more likely you are to be invited to the next level of education and the more attention and money you are given by the department.

On a regular basis, bodies from inside and outside our group evaluate our program to ensure that discipline is being maintained. In this way, our group is linked to other disciplinary groups that hold conferences and publish papers, and this serves to police the area's boundaries. The vast majority of faculty time focuses on elements of our discipline known as core courses.

Pierre Bourdieu produced a number of studies of the French population in which he spoke of *habitus*.[4] In one formulation of this term, he was speaking of the habituation of the poor. He contended that because those who were poor were not exposed to possibilities such as going to university, they simply could not imagine a way out of poverty. They had been habituated to replicate their imprisonment. The lack of options was determinant. Disciplinarity is doing the same thing to our faculty, staff, and students. We are living in intellectual poverty and cannot see the way out. We can only imagine using the building blocks we have been given.

Few people have questioned the need to become more interdisciplinary, but most of us have had little success in making it happen. The simplest reason why is that we do not have additional time to commit to being interdisciplinary while the requirements of our disciplines are continually increasing. By nature, critical thinking and its control systems grow exponentially. Departments replace retiring faculty and maintain old courses rather than retool their working groups to reflect the strengths of the people they have. Deans and administrators stream money based on disciplines, and we sell education in programmatic packages to students, parents, and future employers.

Interdisciplinary projects are an evolutionary threat to the strictures of the disciplines. The system is everywhere fighting to keep us locked behind our walls. There is no doubt that a dynamic educational structure would provide a more robust form of engagement, but we are still turning out students with disciplinary majors using a factory model that took over the universities in order to serve industrial economies. Universities used to be much more open, and degree programs used to be far more expansive. This separation of faculty, staff, and students into camps within which certain sets of information and certain sets of policies define us has created boundaries, which we maintain throughout our careers.

Our students wander the campus with clothing that declares what gang they are with – Engineers, Pre-Med, Chem, Bio, English, Business, Arts, and so on. Intramural sports build teams based on these groups, which only deepens this competition. Fundraising campaigns pit these groups against one another to see who can raise more, and this further deepens the trenches between us. There is nothing wrong with healthy competition, but we should be aware that every aspect of our university works to separate people out and then keep them in line within their own little worlds. This model is designed to eliminate individuality and freedom of expression, which just happens to be the opposite of what we are supposed to be encouraging at university. It also means we are training people not to work well together after university.

Here I believe that administrators must take the lead. Departments or faculties that somehow work in a post-disciplinary manner should be given priority in terms of funding and hiring. Academics will flow toward the areas that allow them to pursue the next big idea. Once scholars have a choice to move into more collaborative modes, students will follow. Unfortunately, many students arrive already indoctrinated into the mob mentality of the disciplines. It starts in high school, but most are still open to interdisciplinarity when they arrive. It is only after we take away all their options and lock them into one set of buildings with one set of courses and one set of colleagues that they lose sight of the world of ideas and become the worker bees of a single, solitary program.

The next step will be to reconnect with the real world. Parents who channel their children into recognizable fields are helping to ossify the disciplines. They feel comfortable when they can name what their children are doing. As a result, students show up on campus ready to be accountants, lawyers, and engineers rather than explorers and inventors. Seventy percent of undergraduate students change their major during their education. Clearly, the streaming we are doing is way off. We need to connect with the community and describe the benefits of a university education and not the perks of joining an intellectual gang. Our current system is a hangover of the guild system from hundreds of years ago and has not been serving our students for a long time.

At the other end of the educational trajectory, we need to engage those who employ our graduates. Whether business, government, or the academy, we need to start a new conversation about the people we need for the future and stop training our people out of their creativity. As I mentioned earlier in this book, our system is producing specialists we neither want nor need. Not surprisingly, many in the private and public sectors have changed their hiring practices and no longer give pride of place to a student who has a perfect 4.0 GPA in a traditional discipline. And who can blame them? That type of performance almost guarantees you a subservient being who will never think of anything new to bring to your group. You would be better off buying a computer than hiring a student trained to regurgitate information.

In the most pernicious outcome of the world of disciplinary thinking, universities train huge numbers of academics for jobs that do not exist. The only reason to do this is to preserve the discipline and to create the illusion of value where there is none. There will always be students who wish to study at the master's or doctoral level as part of their personal journey, but far too many are being encouraged to continue in programs that will cost them tens of thousands of dollars with little prospect of employment. If they stay in academe, they likely face years of teaching a handful of courses while having no voting rights, no benefits, and no control over their assignments. If they leave the academy, the narrowness of their education renders them "over-educated" and undesirable to many employers.

But you might ask: How can one be over-educated? How could more of such an inherently good thing make us less desirable to others? What exactly does this education *do* to people that makes them less valuable than people without education? We tend to gloss over these questions, but the issue impacts lives around the world.

If what we were doing at universities was inherently good and involved a world of free inquiry and creative engagement, being over-educated would be impossible. But what we are doing is indoctrinating people into narrow disciplines so that the way they think is so proscribed that they are seen as useless to their fellow citizens. How does that not cause us alarm? No one is suggesting we are doing this intentionally, but surely we need to ask ourselves whether this type of education is causing more harm than good. If – in a publicly funded institution – we are reducing opportunities for our students and rendering them *less* employable, we are surely perpetrating a kind of fraud. Our fellow citizens help pay the bills, we benefit from the entrenchment of our discipline and continued funding, and the students pay for the privilege. Then, after they pay us with their time and money, the reward is a harder life when they return to the world. If only *we* benefit and everyone else is harmed, there is a serious problem. We must do better.

Of course, this is not new. For years we have spoken of this problem in the academy. We have tried to ensure that our students have the best chance to succeed. We counsel prospective graduate students and give papers and write articles about the dangers of academe, but nothing has changed. Why? Critical thinking presents a world of habituation that does not *allow* us to change. It promotes conditioned minds. In fact, it promotes a type of self-congratulatory stasis that allows us to affirm that we are doing our best when we are actually doing nothing at all. Indeed, taken to its logical extreme, critical thinking for its own survival *needs* things to be bad. A world without things to distrust is anathema for critical thought.

Perhaps if too much education can alienate us from the world of work, there is something we can do when we approach education that will allow us to maintain or heighten our productive, creative, and inventive nature. Creativity experts tend to focus on two areas when discussing the fuel for creative work. In fact, both are part of the same idea. We must be willing to take risks, and we must not be afraid to fail. We have all heard these assertions, and the reason is that they are – in large measure – demonstrably true.

Returning to our common theme – how does a classroom, studio, or lab that is governed by critical thinking treat risk and failure? Critical thought works well with fixed grading systems and established lines of thought, but it deliberately quashes risk-taking by penalizing us for any assertions that can be found lacking. Recall that in any definition we can find in any of the major dictionaries and in textbooks teaching critical thought, the primary function of critical thinking is judgment. Judgment may well be the single greatest enemy of risk-taking and creativity. Moreover, it only stands to reason that the longer we submit ourselves to this system the more likely we are to be risk averse, tentative, and decidedly in-the-box thinkers. We might say highly *disciplined* thinkers.

In his 2005 Stanford University commencement speech, Steve Jobs described his approach to a creative university education. Jobs quit his major and attended classes on a case-by-case basis, following interest and passion alone. A surprising number of our most creative minds find ways to pursue their own path through education. Extracurricular pursuits, option courses, minor programs, course grazing, and projects that involve work off campus all seem to be part of our most innovative thinkers' educational lives. What can we do to support and perhaps even encourage these young minds in their pursuit of the next horizon?

It is a truism in the world of business that you never hire a prospective employee who comes to you with a 4.0 GPA (the highest possible) unless you are looking for a drone. This is because anyone who has a 4.0 has demonstrated not that they will make an exciting new member of the team, but rather that they are the type of person who does anything they are told. Only someone who obediently commits to the discipline can achieve such a grade. Thus, the best that we in the academy have to offer is not what the outside world is looking for when they seek the best people.

Allow me to return for a moment to our discussion of the two branches of education that underpin our current global system. As noted earlier, the ancient Greeks proposed that we commit to two pursuits – *know thyself*, and *care for thyself*. A system that over-educates so as to produce students who, when they achieve the highest levels, become *less* useful to our society runs counter to these original goals. We have become a world obsessed with know thyself and have forgotten about care of thyself.

Recall that the purpose of *care for thyself* was to develop one's talents so as to best serve one's fellow citizens. Our educational system is unbalanced because it has developed too far an isolationist, disciplinary norm that removes students from society and makes it very difficult for them to find their way back.

The solution to this problem is both old and new.

Early models of education stemming from the ancient Greek principles were developed into what came to be known as the liberal arts. The liberal arts are those arts that liberate the individual from ignorance and allow him or her to live as a free citizen. Originally, this area of academe covered the arts *and* the sciences. Balance was key, and students receiving this training were required to work in all areas. It was clear to the elites of the old world, as it is to their fellows today, that a broad education is the best approach to developing the individual. Disciplines are good for worker bees. Those programs do not allow for the development of skills related to self-reflection; they also lack the interdisciplinary view that would allow them to challenge the powers that be. For the global elite, the liberal arts remain the education of choice. Poor and middle-class students get warehoused in large industrial universities. We need to distribute broader education more widely. Students need more dynamic training in order to develop creative thinking.

A recommitment to liberal arts will not, however, be sufficient. The servile arts – those in which we develop ourselves in order to serve our fellow citizens – also need to be given their due. Our world has changed greatly since the first two branches of education were pondered. We do not need to maintain an allegiance to them merely because they came first. But we would do well to recognize that we adopted a system that asserted balance and transformed it into hyper-disciplinary zones of seclusion and that as a result, we all are alienated from our world and ourselves.

A balanced education would require us to attempt to create broader educational experiences. Programs that support the integration of arts and engineering, or science and business, and that begin and then support conversations among all areas on campus offer a way to create thinkers for the twenty-first century. That, or we can continue to offer an experience that is survived rather than celebrated and that produces students who need to take unpaid internships in order to learn what they actually need to know in order to thrive.

For students, this means taking more option courses. An engineer who took an additional year's worth of courses to become a more educated being would be a mighty force on the global market. A dancer who understands economics would break new ground, a doctor who makes films would learn not only science but also human interaction. Of course, the best schools are already doing this type of work. In China, India, and the United States, top-tier programs are running arts programs *within* schools of engineering and medicine.

Years ago, all students on a university campus shared a certain bundle of classes that examined issues of global importance. As we became more isolated, English departments stopped teaching writing, and survey courses were no longer required. The university lost a group of classes that brought all students together. Each discipline began offering courses with names like "Writing for Economics," "Writing for Engineers," or, in some cases, "Writing Across the Disciplines." Research methods became narrowly defined in order to reproduce linear paths.

What we gave up as we retreated further and further into ourselves was the heart of the university. *Universitas*: the whole. The word for university came from this Latin root. To be educated at the university was to engage with the whole – the whole being, the whole body of knowledge, and the whole of society. We have broken apart; we are fragmented, alone, and fearful. We need to reunite our family and ourselves by emphasizing a program of work that is open, creative, and loving. We need universal education for the digital, global, twenty-first century.

Chapter 7

Conclusion

An Open Invitation — Some Final Ideas and Questions

A grandmother was speaking to her young granddaughter. She told the story of the two wolves that live inside us all. The two wolves are constantly in battle to be the one who will dominate our lives. The one wolf is driven by fear, hatred, and violence. The other is governed by love and compassion. The young granddaughter asked, "Which wolf will win?" The grandmother replied, "The one you feed."

This book suggests that we have been feeding the wrong wolf. When we emphasize a critical model, we begin each discussion from a place of suspicion rather than trust. We will always need to balance the best of what open, contributory, creative models have to offer with the benefits of constructive criticism, but I sincerely believe that we should highlight creative rather than critical work at the heart of learning. Critical thinking was never intended to be the central operating system for our thought and for our lives. It was created as a system for testing our contributions to society and for enriching discussions of important issues. *Constructive* criticism has a place in the creative process but should not be our primary mode of operation at the university.

In lieu of a traditional final chapter, I would like to discuss some of the questions and challenges that arise from our discussion. This book has raised more questions than it can reasonably address, and it would be unfortunate if we let ourselves become distracted with the many open-ended questions it has asked. So let us spend some time on areas where this topic would benefit from expansion.

This book has taken a deliberately broad approach to a large topic. As such, it will not please anyone in terms of detail. Please accept this short text as an invitation to take this subject up in a more granular, focused, and connected way, depending on your circumstances. The only way this book could be written for all members of the academy was to make it as open as possible, which means that its scope will be immediately frustrating for those who long for more expansive consideration of the many issues raised. I look forward to hearing the contributions of my colleagues with expertise in the various areas that make up post-secondary education.

I worry that the tone of this text is sometimes too shrill. When attempting to think differently about long-held beliefs, it becomes necessary to speak boldly. I hope this book has opened space for discussions instead of just mimicking the push/pull of critical discourse that I am suggesting we leave behind. If I am correct, the all-pervasive nature of critical discourse will mean that none of us will be able to speak outside its controls for quite some time. I have struggled to do so, and I am certain I have failed much of the time.

This book is intended as a conversation with open terms. The ideas presented here suggest that due to our long-standing commitment to critical thinking, almost everything comes out sounding as if it were a battle of ideas rather than a sharing. There is no real "us versus them." As the cartoon character Pogo once said, "We have met the enemy and he is us." I am every bit as responsible for the problems I suggest we should attempt to fix as anyone else at the university. Our situation is particularly challenging given that faculty, staff, and administrators are overworked and underpaid at a time when I am calling for massive change. My hope is that some of the suggestions I am making can lead to conversations that help make our lives better. We need justice on our campuses, and we are the only ones who can provide it. Positive change cannot help but be good for our students and for society at large.

The frame I use in this book may seem more linear than I intend. Because I am asking a direct question about a very large subject, there is a certain amount of antagonist/protagonist tension in the text. I have worked hard to keep the writing open so as not to turn off readers before they even pick up the book, but I am sure the discussion veers into the antagonistic at times. My only hope is that we can see around those corners to the paths ahead.

My suggestions in this book involve a program to alter the course of our educational system by rebooting the university. There is much work to be done, but we also need to be aware of a particular problem in the university that is exacerbating the problems presented by critical thinking. Over the last several decades, governments have been providing less money for post-secondary education. Parents and students do not want tuition increases, so there is an inherent impasse. The result is that we have a top heavy academy at a time when we are undergoing the most sweeping set of changes in the history of our world. Those at the top of the university food chain appear to the outside world as if they have wonderful jobs, but I believe they are the most overextended generation of academics in history. They are trying to hold together a system designed to be continually replenished by a stream of new scholars. But those new scholars are not being hired in nearly sufficient numbers. And at this time of understaffing, enrolments continue to grow. The toll on the mental and physical health of academics has been devastating. No wonder so many of them are not as prepared as they might be for change in the academy. Again, my hope is that a creative approach will help us come together and address some of these challenges to make our world of work a healthier one.

A note about politics: for years, academics and many in the community at large have believed that critical thinking is somehow connected to a progressive political model. In this perception, critical thinking helps us see through the powerful interests of those who would oppress us – it allows us to fight for our freedom. But if this book is correct – if the forces of critical thinking have been connected to suspicion and to violent attacks on ideas – then nothing could be further from the truth. Critical thinking is far more regressive than creative work and operates – as Plato wanted – as a protective shield that keeps the academy isolated from change while allowing the powerful to control information.

Of course, not all information can be treated creatively to positive effect. Limit cases such as Holocaust denial do not require that a listener offer "yes, and ..." statements. There will be many areas where a creative approach is not warranted. Basic safety, dignity, and respect are required of creative work, and until those elements are in place, we will not be truly functioning as a university. Perhaps, in some extreme cases, creative engagement with unpopular ideas may offer a way to demonstrate productive new ways of thinking, but this is not always so.

During our discussions, I pointed out that in general, people who write about creativity tend to focus on the creation of something *new* that has *value*. Because critical work follows such strict patterns of engagement, it is easier to evaluate than creative work. To foster the latter, colleagues, administrators, and granting agencies will have to make a serious effort. A similar problem arises when faculty consider how to mark creative rather than critical work. Those who work in creative fields already know that truly creative work is extraordinarily competitive; even when we work in a world of sharing and openness, only the very best ideas make it to the stage, the concert hall, the gallery, the exhibition. A move toward the creative will not collapse standards, it will strengthen them.

We should ask, to what extent would a move toward creativity offer a rebalancing, which could focus not on replacing critical thinking but rather on reconfiguring its position in our work? If the two modes were balanced, what would the result look like? The discussion in this area often involves examples of constructive criticism and its power to take the elements of the creative process to the next level of expression. In all of the cases I have seen, I would suggest that less than 10 percent of our time should be spent on this type of critical work. That includes the extremes such as the famous Pixar trash sessions and the editing of critical work. Of course, these ratios will vary depending on the given project, but my understanding is that critical work should play an important but minor role in the life of learning.

Creative work requires more effort and more vulnerability than critical work. That is one reason why there are so many critics and so few artists. Fully creative work requires all of our being and as such will meet with resistance from those who do not wish to open themselves to the conversation and to contribute something of themselves to it. Critical thinking allows us to pretend we are separate and objective. It makes us superior. We sit in judgment rather than joining the people. Creative work is a social and compassionate practice.

My argument against the privileged position that critical thinking enjoys should not be mistaken for an attack on logic, rhetoric, or analytical thinking. Rather, this book asserts that we have accepted a particular mode of work as part of an overall approach to life. That approach came from violent origins and was strengthened by those who contended that human beings needed to be constrained and controlled in order to live the best lives. This idea has nothing to do with philosophical work. But I am not suggesting we move away from the study of logic – in fact, the study of logic in departments of philosophy should be seen as one way to improve creative facility in the same way that literacy and numeracy do. Likewise, work on analytical reading and writing and a greater emphasis on rhetoric are excellent ways to avoid the hostility of critical thinking while maintaining the benefits of structured intellectual engagement.

It is important that I expose my bias within the academy. I began my working life as an artist, trained as an academic, was tenured as an English professor, and then made a mid-career shift that brought me back to the fine arts. So I may well be biased against the more critical world I left behind.

Perhaps I was ill suited for critical scholarship and am creating straw men in order to work out my own personal concerns, in much in the way Plato was distracted by his very real love for his teacher. I do not believe this to be the case, but I must admit the possibility.

For those who work on creativity and the arts, the proclivity of some people to equate the casual with the creative is a source of great frustration. These people are using creative thinking to get away with a type of mental laziness that critical thinking uproots. In my experience, this is not the case with genuine creative work, because artists and audiences vet it so ruthlessly; but around the edges there is always the potential to call something creative that is merely half-formed. The conflation of the casual and the creative will necessarily be of utmost importance in any move toward increased creative work in the university. Recall our definition: to be creative is to create something new that has value. Lazy work does not meet that standard.

Science tells us that creative people are happier than their critical counterparts. Even so, we should be careful not to view creativity as embracing a Pollyanna view of the world – that is, as an excuse to ignore real-world problems. The critical mind keeps us suspicious all of the time, relentlessly searching for problems. When we de-emphasize the critical mind, all of our problems will not go away. Nor does creativity equate with positive thinking. When moving to a more creative model we will need to ensure that our creativity is solution-oriented and not merely an abstract set of distractions.

At the start of this book, I tried to provide a historical overview of the history of thought relevant to our discussion. Whenever we write about intellectual history in the West we must discuss the Roman Catholic Church, particularly the centuries between Constantine and the Renaissance. When we examine these periods, and level accusations at "the Church" for its rule and regulation of people, we make it sound as if the two were separate entities when in fact, at that time, society *was* the Church and the Church *was* society. When writing about the Church of that time, we always run the risk of oversimplification.

While we are on this topic, let us take a moment to consider religion. Given that I spent so much time discussing the ideas of Christopher Hitchens (and to a lesser extent Richard Dawkins), I believe it important to offer a clarification about creativity and religion. It can seem at times that religion is anti-creativity, but the truth is far more complicated. Almost all religions contain forces that have attempted to repress creative work, but those forces do not speak for all of the followers of any set of beliefs; indeed, within any religion there are creative people who often work at odds with those for whom faith provides great, creative inspiration. Most major religions have strong strains of creative work in their histories.

As we move toward a new way of working on campus, certain disciplines may encounter greater barriers to access when it comes to collaboration and integration with the broader public. My own experience is primarily in the arts and humanities, where much of our work is – or could be – accessible to the public. Someone working in advanced theoretical physics may have a harder time explaining what she or he has been thinking about lately. As such, some areas may have an easier time reaching out to others in interdisciplinary projects. Some of this openness, then, is an illusion, and greater understanding of complex work in areas such as music may only be found through effort. If we were all trained in the way suggested in this book, we would all have the skills to describe our work to one another. In the near term, and in nearly all cases, work on knowledge transfer will be important in order to make possible the collaboration and connection I describe.

On the topic of communication, I should note that during my many conversations at conferences and as part of public speaking events about the material covered in this book, I have often been asked, "What type of language can we use to begin working creatively rather than critically?" This is an excellent question and one I suggest should be the topic of much more research. The short answer is that it is not a question of language, but of tactics. When someone speaks, do not sit listening for something you disagree with, note it, and then attack. Hear the whole speech, reflect, and consider whether you have anything to add. If you do not, why not consider saying nothing? The most dangerous aspect of critical thinking is its propensity to move into the realm of *ad hominem* attack. Too often we hear responses to discussions that suggest moral evaluations of the individual speaking because of what they said. When we operate in that way, all possibility of dynamic engagement is lost. Responses like "When I hear you speak of x, it makes me think of y" are more contributory and should prove more in keeping with a creative approach. Our colleagues in psychology – particularly group psychology – have much to offer us here. When it comes to a longer answer, I suspect that detailed work in the areas of logic, rhetoric, and formal analysis will provide many useful options that take us out of the violent language of attack that pervades critical thinking and into forms that can sustain and promote complexity, nuance, and clarity.

In various parts of this book, I have addressed issues that relate to tenure as a means of organizing university work. I feel it important to be very clear on this most important issue. Two major items need attending to if my ideas are to be put into practice. First, we have to recognize that creativity requires open access to information. All attempts to restrict, limit, or bias data are anathema to any type of creative work. Thus, the system of tenure and rigorous reviews of research results are of utmost importance. In the case of research evaluation, it has long been known that peer review is very good at maintaining the status quo and keeping out groundbreaking research. In Canada, the major funding bodies rather calmly advise grant applicants that bold new ideas are unlikely to be supported. We need to look again at what blind review can do for us and ensure that those who conduct reviews are also placed on review. Demonstration of bias should be determined blindly and incorporated into the system. As important as tenure is, we must admit that it is currently operating in ways that do not serve us. Too often, tenure does not protect ideas and research but instead protects jobs for people who are working hard to block new discoveries. Those who wish to end their careers without acknowledging the techno-logical revolution are chief among these. To remain current as academics, at the very least we must be scholars of the twenty-first century.

The clogged tenure system is behind the flight of leading researchers from our campuses. We are often told that star academics leave for the money, but those who pursue a life in academe have demonstrated that ideas and not money are their primary concern. They leave because the current system does not protect and nurture thought but instead guarantees long-term employment to a large number of unpleasant and unproductive faculty. Of course sometimes that faculty is unproductive because they are stranded in departments with no new hiring and increasing student enrol-ment, facing a new world they are struggling to engage. Something has to give. The situation is complicated, but what is clear is that tenure must be re-evaluated so that we do not lose it to the proverbial death by a thousand cuts. Research has shown that the most negative people in organizations are the ones who work hardest to influence hiring. That finding has serious implications for our current system.

I would like to close in the same way I began – with an invitation. This book is intended as a thought experiment. It has been written to allow for the broadest possible readership. The benefit of having a book that is acces-sible to all is that we can use this opening as a starting point for our own, more detailed discussions on our campuses.

Throughout my work on this project, I have been warned repeatedly that this is a fool's mission, a career killer, even an act of madness. I have been warned that I will be attacked for some of the suggestions in this book. My hope is because I have provided a text that is so simple – and thus so easily attacked – it will not be worth anyone's time to give it the type of violent critical attention that will be unhelpful. Rather, I hope we can have a good long discussion about ways we might be able to live more open, contributory, and creative lives. If we can do so, we will really have something that is new and of value to pass to the next generation of scholars and to the world in which we live.

Thank you for taking the time to read these words. I hope you will join me in this thought experiment.

Notes

Chapter 1

1 Readers interested in Ken Robinson's ideas on creativity should also consider his *The Element;* and also his *Finding Your Element*. Written after his celebrated TED talk in 2006, these books use anecdotes, studies, statistics, and established success stories to demonstrate the practical benefits of a creative education and a life of passion. With the same balance of accessibility, intellectual rigour, and cultural relevancy that made his TED talk famous, Robinson continues this critical through line with these follow-up efforts.

Chapter 2

1 See Plato's *Phaedo* for his account of Socrates's death. Readers interested in exploring classical texts related to Socrates, Plato, and Aristotle will find everything they need online. There are also countless editions of the works. In all cases, the use of "Stephanus" notation allows you to look up the same thing in different sources. The system of notation comes from an influential publication in 1578.

2 For more on Plato's exclusion of the poets, see *The Republic*, Book X.

3 See Aristotle's *Politics*, Book II, for further discussion of the Platonic conception of an ideal state.

4 See Foucault, *The History of Sexuality*, vol. 3.

5 Beyond *The History of Sexuality*, vol. 3, readers interested in Foucault's applications of the Delphic principle "know thyself" and the Socratic "care of the self" should consider his "Technologies of the Self." Derived from a seminar Foucault gave at the University of Vermont in 1982, this late lecture elucidates his earlier conception of these Classical tenets and explains the disproportionate privileging of "know thyself" in contemporary society.

6 For more on Socrates's refutation of sophistry, see Plato's *The Sophist*.

7 The story of Thrasymachus is told in *The Republic*, Book I.

8 Readers interested in the historical and contemporary implications of the Thrasymachus episode in *The Republic* should consider Saxonhouse's in-depth study of free speech during the period, *Free Speech and Democracy in Ancient Athens*. Through exegesis, historical events, and the ideologies of the age, Saxonhouse presents a

thorough and compelling depiction of Ancient Greek political structures and social sentiments. Her study also offers an ideal contextual framework for evaluating Thrasymachus as a potential symbol of free speech, both then and now.

9 Readers interested in Plato's hierarchy of education should also consider *The Laws* for further development of the theme.

10 Readers interested in the legacy of Ancient Greek comedies should consider Olson, *Broken Laughter*. Comedy was the favoured genre at the time and thousands of comedic plays were produced, but barely a dozen survive intact. For that reason, and because we have lost Aristotle's appraisal of the genre in *The Poetics*, Greek tragedy has risen to disproportionate prominence in modern times and altered our collective perceptions of theatrical forms. In his anthology and critical text, Olson helps bring these lost works and their cultural context to light.

11 Aristotle most famously and explicitly champions the arts in *The Poetics*.

12 Readers interested in the preservation of overthrown societies in the Roman Empire should also consider *The Oxford Handbook of Social Relations in the Roman World*. In this thorough study of Roman customs and cultures, editor Michael Peachin maintains a broad scope and observes how different cultures were retained and represented in the Roman Empire. In Part VI, "Societies within the Roman Community," the continued influence of Greek, Christian, and Jewish societies is closely examined. This integrated approach emphasizes the points of convergence between the Roman Empire and other cultures, as well as their shared customs.

13 For examples of Roman tragedy's reliance on violence, see Seneca's adaptations of *The Trojan Women, Oedipus, Medea, The Mad Hercules, The Phoenician Women, Phaedra, Agamemnon,* and *Thyestes*.

14 For more on the role of debate in Roman society, consider Donfried, ed., *The Romans Debate*. By returning Roman texts to their original social and cultural context, the contributors to this anthology emphasize the formal, rhetorical, and functional parallels among these apparently dissimilar works. In looking at historical and sociological factors, structure and rhetoric, and Roman theology, editor Donfried takes a broad approach to the subject, one that emphasizes the pervasive influence of debate in Roman culture.

15 Only fragments of Epicurus's many works now survive. However, the philosophical tenets of Epicureanism can still be found in *The Principal Doctrines*.

16 For more on the influence of *Piers Plowman* on the 1381 Peasant Revolt, see Galloway, "Making History Legal." In that chapter, Galloway explores the social implications of *Piers Plowman* and how this creative text helped lay the foundations for great social change. In this historical case study, Galloway alludes to the direct relationship between creative thought and practical applications.

17 Readers interested in Christopher Marlowe's theatrical innovations should also consider Russ McDonald's "Marlowe and Style." In that chapter, McDonald returns Marlowe to his historical context and reads his dramas through the theatrical milieu of sixteenth-century England. By considering Marlowe's formal and stylistic innovations, such as the use of blank verse, through the practices of the age, McDonald emphasizes Marlowe's status as an artistic innovator, lateral thinker, and creative contributor.

18 Those interested in the implications of *Beowulf*'s debatable provenance should also consider Orchard, *A Critical Companion to Beowulf*. In his examination of the tale's textual history, style, structure, and social order, Orchard acknowledges the layered and revisionary aspects of this canonical work. Asserting that *Beowulf* as we know it

is the Christian reworking of a pagan tale (130), Orchard underscores the instability of meaning in this foundational text and the continued possibility for creative revision or reinterpretation.

19 Readers interested in William Caxton's importation of Gutenberg's print technology should also consider Blake, *William Caxton and English Literary Culture*. Blake's study looks at the spread of printing in England during the fifteenth century and Caxton's influence on the production and dissemination of texts. By exploring these technological developments and their broader social implications, Blake demonstrates Caxton's influence on the changing cultural landscape of his time and the opportunities for new creative freedom.

20 For more on linguistic and grammatical freedom in the Elizabethan period, see Cercignani, *Shakespeare's Works and Elizabethan Pronunciation*. Cercignani's exploration of Shakespeare's innovative approach to language concurrently charts the development of Modern English. Writing in a time when language was not fettered by rigid standards and limitations, Shakespeare was free to compose without linguistic constrictions.

21 For a point of entry into Enlightenment ideology, see Spinoza, *Ethics*, Newton, *Philosophiæ Naturalis Principia Mathematica*, or Voltaire, *Candide*. Although these works are only representative and span time and place, they help establish the philosophical and scientific groundwork for the intellectual age.

22 Anyone interested in the historical privileging of scientists in French society may want to consider Lynn, *Popular Science and Public Opinion in Eighteenth-Century France*. In his study of the prevalence and popularization of science in eighteenth-century France, Lynn demonstrates how the scientist became an honoured figure. This privileging of science and scientists recalls the same Platonic ideals from *The Republic* and suggests a point of ideological connection between the two periods.

23 See Rousseau's *Confessions*.

24 For further information on Nietzsche's approach to art, see his *The Birth of Tragedy*. In this early work, Nietzsche explores the origins, forms, and functions of ancient Greek tragedy.

25 Nietzsche's attitudes toward Judeo-Christianity are also captured in *On the Genealogy of Morals*.

26 Wittgenstein significantly explored the importance of language in the *Tractatus Logico-Philosophicus* in 1921. The title is a nod toward Spinoza's *Tractatus Theologico-Politicus* and alludes to the critical continuity between the two.

27 See, for example, Heidegger's "Letter on Humanism, 1949" for his views on the functions, structures, and systems of language as they relate to his theories in *Being and Time*.

28 Readers interested in the notion of the "linguistic turn" should also consider Rorty, *The Linguistic Turn*. In this anthology, the changed state of late and postmodern philosophy is attributed to a new approach to language. By focusing on the relationship between philosophy and language, this landmark collection of essays both identified and contributed to the critical and philosophical *zeitgeist*. For further information on the subject from a twenty-first-century perspective, readers should also consider Clark, *History, Theory, Text*.

29 Those interested in the critical and philosophical innovations of Heidegger and Wittgenstein should also consider Braver, *Groundless Grounds: A Study of Wittgenstein and Heidegger,* in which the author correlates the ideas of these formative philosophers. In doing so, he observes their individual and collective contributions to

the critical reconsideration of language in the modern and postmodern periods. Using ontology, thought processes, definitions of philosophy, and human action as points of entry, Braver considers how both philosophers use language to create and interpret new meaning.

30 Readers interested in the use of language as a means of retaining power should also consider Mooney and Peccei, *Language, Society and Power*, in which the authors examine language as it relates to areas such as politics, gender, ethnicity, social class, and the media. Casting their net wide, they consider the far-reaching implications of language in society. In doing so, they demonstrate how language affects all facets of life and is often and effectively used by those in control as a means of retaining power.

31 Readers interested in the use of language as a tool of oppression should also consider Bosmajian, *The Language of Oppression*. Through significant examples of language's subversive influence in history, the author explores the dangerous effects of violent or manipulative rhetoric.

32 For the biblical depiction of the Tower of Babel, see Genesis 11:1–9.

33 See MacLean, *The Triune Brain in Evolution*.

Chapter 3

1 Readers interested in the culture of debate and the Oxford Union should also consider Walter, *The Oxford Union*, and Graham, *Playing at Politics*. Both texts explore the structure and cultural associations of this highly esteemed debating society. While Walter traces the Oxford Union's historical lineage, Graham explores its politics and prestige through social anthropology. Taken together, these two works construct a detailed depiction of this legendary society and the continued privileging of debate.

2 See Mann, *The Quotable Hitchens*. Martin Amis, British novelist and one of Hitchens's lifelong friends, made a similar comparison between Hitchens and Cicero. In his foreword to Mann's book, Amis asserts that "in debate, no matter what the motion, I would back him against Cicero, against Demosthenes" (viii).

3 To view the Hitchens brothers' famous debate, see the Michigan Centre for Inquiry's archival footage, available on YouTube at "Brothers Debate God and War," www.youtube.com/watch?v=1XHv7IQCg-w.

4 For Sontag's exploration of the stigmatization of illness and the alienating effects of language, see her *Illness as Metaphor* (1978) as well as her follow-up text, *AIDS and Its Metaphors* (1988). For her views on social distancing and the silencing of subjectivity, see her *On Photography* (1977) and *Regarding the Pain of Others* (2003). As an artist, activist, and academic, Sontag used her work as a platform for exploring the creative and practical implications of social attitudes and behaviours.

5 For example, see Pinker, *The Better Angels of Our Nature*. In this text, he brings his psychological, linguistic, scientific, and authorial expertise to the study of violence in society. Through a broader scope and a more holistic approach, his academic interest in the subject takes on greater social implications.

6 Cornel West's impressive academic career has been punctuated by a number of important and formative texts. As a prominent representative for social justice, racial equality, and equal rights, he has spent years fighting for the rights of others. Through notable works such as *Race Matters* (1994) and his recent book with co-

author Tavis Smiley, *The Rich and the Rest of Us* [2012]), West has given a voice to those who are often silenced.

7 Canadian communications theorist Marshall McLuhan was a pioneer of information technology and helped cultivate emergent forms of digital exchanges in the modern world. Through landmark works such as *The Medium Is the Massage, War and Peace in the Global Village,* and (with Bruce R. Powers) *The Global Village* (1989), he offered a conceptual framework for the bourgeoning field of digital communication. He viewed the world as a single interconnected community transformed by communication technology, and explored the greater social implications of these changes.

8 In both her life and her writing, bell hooks is a champion for racial, gender, educational, and social equality. Through texts such as *Feminist Theory* and *Writing Beyond Race,* she explores the effects of systemic oppression and marginalization in society.

9 As one of this century's most formative thinkers, Chomsky has helped define contemporary approaches to language, social structures, and information systems. His impressive critical oeuvre is highlighted by such notable titles as *Syntactic Structures* and (with Edward Herman) *Manufacturing Consent.*

10 Fukuyama's academic contributions have helped define the field of political science. His landmark text, *The End of History and the Last Man* (1992), projects a theoretical "end of history" through the pervasion of Western culture on a global scale. Fukuyama and his work are marked by a refined social consciousness and a sensitivity to the broader implications of ideological changes in the world.

11 For Steve Job's commencement address, see "'You've Got to Find What You Love,' Jobs Says."

12 A quote attributed to Jobs that has gone viral. Visit en.wikiquote.org/wiki/Steve _Jobs.

13 See Hitchens, *Why Orwell Matters.*

14 For more on Orwell's social awareness and politicized approach to writing, see his *Why I Write.*

15 See Hitchens, *The Missionary Position.*

16 See Hitchens, *No One Left to Lie To.*

17 See Hitchens, *God Is Not Great;* and Hitchens and Wilson, *Is Christianity Good for the World?*

18 See Nietzsche, *Beyond Good and Evil,* s. 146: "Battle not with monsters, lest ye become a monster, and if you gaze into the abyss, the abyss gazes also into you."

19 For more on Hitchens's response to the Rushdie case, see his "Now, Who Will Speak for Rushdie?"

20 Readers interested in the academy's response to the Rushdie case should also consider Hitchens's *Vanity Fair* article "Assassins of the Mind." In this 2009 retrospective, he recalls the popular apathy toward Rushdie at the time of his 1989 *fatwā* and points to Sontag as one of the few who defended the writer.

21 See Hitchens, *Love, Poverty, and War.* In the first section of that book, "Love," he reflects on his most beloved writers and praises their artistic contributions.

22 For exemplary texts, see Ken Robinson's *The Arts in Schools* or bell hooks's *Teaching Critical Thinking* and *Teaching Community.*

23 See Dawkins, *The Magic of Reality.*

24 Mazella, *The Making of Modern Cynicism.* Readers interested in the rise of the cynic should consider this fascinating book. Beginning with ancient philosophical con-

ceptions of cynicism, Mazella returns the role to its original cultural context and challenges modern understandings of the cynic. Examining primary texts from different time periods, he makes a compelling case for the rehabilitation of the cynic and a reconsideration of the cynic's role in modern criticism.

Chapter 4

1 See Bourdieu's original French text *La Distinction* or its later English translation.
2 See Florida's *Who's Your City?* and *Cities and the Creative Class.*
3 For more on the formalist desire to "make it strange," see essays from Russian formalists, such as Viktor Shklovsky's "Art as Technique," Boris Tomashevsky's "Thematics," and Eikhenbaum's "The Theory of the 'Formal Method.'" These essays are included in many anthologies as well as being available in translation online.
4 Readers interested in the notion of "hermeneutics of suspicion" should also consider Ricoeur's formative text, *Freud and Philosophy.* Ricoeur's reserach reaches beyond the confines of psychoanalysis to confront the "grand philosophy of language" and the emergent practice of a "hermeneutics of suspicion" in the modern age. For further commentary on this subject, see also Alison Scott-Baumann's *Ricoeur and the Hermeneutics of Suspicion.*
5 See Bradt, *Acing the Only Three True Job Interview Questions.*
6 See Goldberg, "Materialism Is Bad for You, Studies Say." Readers interested in the effect of materialism on human development and emotional well-being should also consider Diener and Biswas-Diener, *Happiness.* In this rich psychological study, fellow psychologists and father and son Ed Diener and Robert Biswas-Diener explore scientific conceptions of contentment and offer practical solutions. Through their consideration of happiness as a biological, social, environmental, and personal creation, they offer diverse strategies for achieving greater happiness.
7 Readers interested in positive psychology should consider Seligman and Csikszentmihalyi, "Positive Psychology: An Introduction." In this foundational description, the authors introduce positive psychology and define the terms of this emerging subject. Characterized in this introduction by an emphasis on subjective experience, positive psychology reflects changing attitudes about emotional well-being and personal response in the twenty-first century.

Chapter 5

1 See the first section of Kierkegaard, *Either/Or,* "Diapsalmata."
2 See Jacobs, *The Death and Life of Great American Cities.*
3 See Lyotard, *The Postmodern Condition.*
4 Readers interested in the "sage on the stage" approach to teaching should also consider Allison King's "From Sage on the Stage to Guide on the Side." In this article, King observes the paradigm shift from the more declamatory "sage on the stage" approach of traditional educators to the collaborative "guide on the side" format. For more on this teaching strategy and the changed approach to instruction, see also Halpern, *Changing College Classrooms.*
5 See McWilliam, "Unlearning How to Teach."

6 See Robinson, "Ken Robinson Says Schools Kill Creativity," "Bring On the Learning Revolution!," and "How to Escape Education's Death Valley."
7 See Gladwell, *Outliers*; Pink, *A Whole New Mind*; and Florida, ed., *Industrializing Knowledge*.
8 See Isaacson, *Steve Jobs*; and Aronson, *Bill Gates*.
9 See Robinson, "Ken Robinson Says Schools Kill Creativity."
10 See Robinson, "Ken Robinson Says Schools Kill Creativity."
11 See Hall, *The Academic Self*; and Hall, *The Academic Community*.
12 See Darwin's foundational text from 1859, *On the Origin of Species*.
13 See Paglia, *Sex and Violence, or Nature and Art*.
14 See David Lodge's Campus Trilogy. See also Amis, *Lucky Jim*.
15 For many, Greenblatt will be known for his central role in the movement known as New Historicism. For more on that, see Veeser, ed., *The New Historicism*. This collection, which includes viewpoints on the subject from celebrated theorists such as Stephen Greenblatt, Catherine Gallagher, and Stephen Bann, captures a turning point in contemporary cultural criticism. See also Greenblatt and Gallagher, *Practicing New Historicism*. In that text, Greenblatt and Gallagher return to the influential concept and consider its changed implications in the twenty-first century. For Greenblatt's move into what I see as a radically "hospitable" form of work, see his *Hamlet in Purgatory*; *Will in the World*; and *The Swerve*. In these books we have a new form of public scholarship that combines rigorous research with personal detail. The New Historicism was marked by a tendency to use the personal, and it is easy to see the development from Greenblatt's earlier work to these later, more popular texts.
16 For the text of Pausch's famous lecture, see *The Last Lecture*.
17 For Florida's conception of the emergent creative class, see his *The Rise of the Creative Class*; and also his *The Flight of the Creative Class*.
18 For Pink's response to the current university structure, see his *Drive*.
19 For more on Geist's work as a proponent of open access, see his *The Copyright Pentalogy*. For Lessig's views on shared access, see his *The Future of Ideas*; and also his *Free Culture*.

Chapter 6

1 For a discussion of liberal education, see Mulcahy, *The Educated Person*. Readers interested in the structure and tenets of liberal education should also consider Mulcahy's *The Educated Person*. Taking a pragmatic approach, Mulcahy considers the usefulness and applications of liberal education at every level of academic study. Triangulating three distinct perspectives on the subject, he takes a broad approach to the history, structure, and future of liberal education.
2 Readers interested in the work of Wade Davis should also consider his *Light at the Edge of the World*.
3 Pearson and Porath, *The Cost of Bad Behavior*.
4 For more on Bourdieu's conception of "habitus," see his *Outline of a Theory of Practice*.

Bibliography

Please note: For works by Plato and Aristotle readers can begin with online texts. There are a number of printed versions of each. All versions are united by the use of so-called "Stephanus" notation after the famed 1573 Stephanus edition. Reliable electronic editions for initial consultation can be found at Project Gutenberg at http://www.gutenberg.org or the Perseus Project at http://www.perseus.tufts.edu.

Amis, Kingsley. *Lucky Jim*. New York: Penguin, 1954.

Aristotle. *The Poetics*.

———. *Politics*, Book II.

Aronson, Marc. *Bill Gates*. New York: Viking, 2009.

Blake, N.F. *William Caxton and English Literary Culture*. London: Hambledon Press, 1991.

Bonhoeffer, Dietrich. *Letters and Papers from Prison*. London: Touchstone, 1997.

Bosmajian, Haig A. *The Language of Oppression*. New York: Public Affairs Press, 1974.

Bourdieu, Pierre. *Distinction: A Social Critique of the Judgement of Taste*. New York: Routledge, 2010.

———. *Outline of a Theory of Practice*. Cambridge: Cambridge University Press, 1977.

Bradt, George. "Acing the Only Three True Job Interview Questions." *Forbes Magazine*, 2 January 2013.

Braver, Lee. *Groundless Grounds: A Study of Wittgenstein and Heidegger*. Cambridge, MA: MIT Press, 2012.

Cercignani, Fausto. *Shakespeare's Works and Elizabethan Pronunciation*. Oxford: Clarendon, 1981.

Chomsky, Noam. *Syntactic Structures* [1951]. London: De Gruyter Mouton, 2012.

Clark, Elizabeth A. *History, Theory, Text: Historians and the Linguistic Turn*. Cambridge, MA: Harvard University Press, 2004.

Darwin, Charles. *On the Origin of Species* [1859]. New York: Signet Classics, 2009.

Davis, Wade. *Light at the Edge of the World: A Journey Through the Realm of Vanishing Cultures*. Vancouver: Douglas & McIntyre, 2007.

Dawkins, Richard. *The Magic of Reality: How We Know What's Really True*. New York: Free Press, 2012.

Diener, Ed, and Robert Biswas-Diener. *Happiness: Unlocking the Mysteries of Psychological Wealth*. Hoboken, NJ: Wiley-Blackwell, 2008.

Donfried, Karl P., ed. *The Romans Debate*. Grand Rapids, MI: Baker Academic, 1991.

Eikhenbaum, Boris Mikhailovich. "The Theory of the 'Formal Method'" [1926]. letras
.cabaladada.org/letras/theory_fomal_method.pdf

Epicurus. *The Principal Doctrines*. www.epicurus.info/etexts/PD.html

Florida, Richard. *Cities and the Creative Class*. New York: Routledge, 2005.

———. *The Flight of the Creative Class: The New Global Competition for Talent*. New
York: HarperCollins, 2007.

———, ed. *Industrializing Knowledge: University–Industry Linkages in Japan and the
United States*. Cambridge, MA: MIT Press, 1999.

———. *The Rise of the Creative Class: And How It's Transforming Work, Leisure, Community and Everyday Life*. New York: Perseus Book Group, 2002.

———. *Who's Your City? How the Creative Economy Is Making Where to Live the Most
Important Decision of Your Life*. New York: Basic Books, 2008.

Foucault, Michel. *The History of Sexuality*, vol. 3: *The Care of Self*. Translated by Robert
Hurley. London: Penguin, 1998.

———. "Technologies of the Self." In *Technologies of the Self: A Seminar with Michel
Foucault*. Edited by Luther H. Martin, Patrick H. Hutton, and Huck Guttman. Am-
herst: University of Massachusetts Press, 1988. 16–49.

Fukuyama, Francis. *The End of History and the Last Man*. New York: Free Press, 1992.

Galloway, Andrew. "Making History Legal: *Piers Plowman* and the Rebels of Fourteenth-
Century England." In *William Langland's Piers Plowman: A Book of Essays*. Edited
by Kathleen M. Hewett-Smith. New York: Routledge, 2001.

Geist, Michael. *The Copyright Pentalogy: How the Supreme Court of Canada Shook the
Foundations of Canadian Copyright Law*. Ottawa: University of Ottawa Press, 2013.

Gladwell, Malcolm. *Outliers: The Story of Success*. New York: Little, Brown, 2008.

Goldberg, Carey. "Materialism Is Bad for You, Studies Say." *New York Times*, 8 February
2006.

Graham, Fiona. *Playing at Politics: An Ethnology of the Oxford Union*. Edinburgh: Dune-
din, 2005.

Greenblatt, Stephen. *Hamlet in Purgatory*. Princeton: Princeton University Press, 2013.

———. *The Swerve*. New York: W.W. Norton, 2012.

———. *Will in the World*. New York: W.W. Norton, 2005.

Greenblatt, Stephen, and Catherine Gallagher. *Practicing New Historicism*. Chicago:
University of Chicago Press, 2000.

Hall, Donald Eugene. *The Academic Community: A Manual for Change*. Columbus:
Ohio State University Press, 2007.

———. *The Academic Self: An Owner's Manual*. Columbus: Ohio State University Press,
2002.

Halpern, Diane F. *Changing College Classrooms: New Teaching and Learning Strategies
for an Increasingly Complex World*. San Francisco: Jossey-Bass, 1994.

Heidegger, Martin. *Being and Time*. Translated by John Stambaugh. Albany: SUNY
Press, 2010.

———. "Letter on Humanism, 1949." In *Martin Heidegger: Basic Writings*. Edited and
translated by David Farrell Krell. New York: Harper, 2008.

Herman, Edward, and Noam Chomsky. *Manufacturing Consent: The Political Economy of the Mass Media*. New York: Pantheon, 2002.

Hitchens, Christopher. "Assassins of the Mind." *Vanity Fair,* February 2009.

———. *God Is Not Great: How Religion Poisons Everything*. New York: Twelve, 2007.

———. *Love, Poverty, and War: Journeys and Essays*. New York: Nation, 2004.

———. *The Missionary Position: Mother Teresa in Theory and Practice*. New York: Twelve, 2012.

———. *No One Left to Lie To: The Values of the Worst Family*. London: Verso, 2000.

———. "Now, Who Will Speak for Rushdie?" *New York Times,* 17 February 1989.

———. *Why Orwell Matters*. New York: Basic Books, 2003.

Hitchens, Christopher, and Peter Hitchens. "Brothers Debate God and War." www .youtube.com/watch?v=1XHv7IQCg-w

Hitchens, Christopher, and Douglas Wilson. *Is Christianity Good for the World? A Debate*. Moscow: Canon Press, 2009.

hooks, bell. *Feminist Theory: From Margin to Center*. Boston: South End Press, 1984.

———. *Teaching Community: A Pedagogy of Hope*. New York: Routledge, 2003.

———. *Teaching Critical Thinking: Practical Wisdom*. New York: Routledge, 2010.

———. *Writing Beyond Race: Living Theory and Practice*. New York: Routledge, 2013.

Hughes, William. *Critical Thinking: An Introduction to the Basic Skills*. Peterborough, ON: Broadview Press, 2000.

Isaacson, Walter. *Steve Jobs*. New York: Simon & Schuster, 2011.

Jacobs, Jane. *The Death and Life of Great American Cities*. New York: Vintage, 1992.

Jobs, Steve. "Wikiquote." en.wikiquote.org/wiki/Steve_Jobs

———. "'You've Got to Find What You Love.'" *Stanford Report,* 14 June 2005.

Kaye, Sharon M. *Critical Thinking: A Beginner's Guide*. Bolinda Introduction to Critical Thinking. London: Oneworld, 2009.

Kierkegaard, Søren. *Either/Or: A Fragment of Life*. New York: Penguin, 2003.

King, Allison. "From Sage on the Stage to Guide on the Side." *College Teaching* 41, no. 1 (1993): 30–35.

Lessig, Lawrence. *Free Culture: How Big Media Uses Technology and the Law to Lock Down Culture and Control Creativity*. London: Penguin, 2004.

———. *The Future of Ideas: The Fate of the Commons in a Connected World*. New York: Vintage, 2002.

Lodge, David. *The Campus Trilogy: Changing Places, Small World, Nice Work*. New York: Penguin, 2011.

Lynn, Michael R. *Popular Science and Public Opinion in Eighteenth-Century France*. Manchester: Manchester University Press, 2006.

Lyotard, Jean-François. *The Postmodern Condition: A Report on Knowledge*. Translated by Geoffrey Bennington and Brian Massumi. Minneapolis: University of Minnesota Press, 1984.

MacLean, Paul D. *The Triune Brain in Evolution: Role in Paleocerebral Functions*. New York: Plenum Press, 1990.

Mann, Windsor. *The Quotable Hitchens: From Alcohol to Zionism: The Very Best of Christopher Hitchens*. Philadelphia: De Capo, 2011.

Mazella, David. *The Making of Modern Cynicism*. Charlottesville: University of Virginia Press, 2007.

McDonald, Russ. "Marlowe and Style." In *The Cambridge Companion to Christopher Marlowe*. Edited by Patrick Cheney. Cambridge: Cambridge University Press, 2006. 55–69.

McLuhan, Marshall, and Quentin Fiore. *The Medium Is the Massage: An Inventory of Effects*. New York: Ginko Press, 2001.

———. *War and Peace in the Global Village*. New York: Ginko Press, 2001.

McLuhan, Marshall, and Bruce R. Powers. *The Global Village: Transformations in World Life and Media in the 21st Century*. Oxford: Oxford University Press, 1989.

McWilliam, Erica. "Unlearning How to Teach." *Innovations in Education and Teaching International* 45, no. 3 (2008): 263–69.

Mooney, Annabelle, and Jean Stilwell Peccei. *Language, Society and Power: An Introduction*. New York, Routledge, 2010.

Moran, Joe. *Interdisciplinarity*. 2nd ed. New York: Routledge, 2010.

Mulcahy, D.G. *The Educated Person: Toward a New Paradigm for Liberal Education*. Lanham: Rowman & Littlefield, 2008.

Newton, Isaac. *Philosopiae Naturalis Principia Mathematica*. Cambridge, MA: Harvard University Press, 1972.

Nietzsche, Friedrich. *Beyond Good and Evil*. Translated by Walter Kaufmann. New York: Vintage, 1989.

———. *The Birth of Tragedy*. Translated by Douglas Smith. Oxford: Oxford University Press, 2008.

———. *On the Genealogy of Morals*. Translated by Walter Kaufmann. New York: Vintage, 1989.

Olson, S. Douglas. *Broken Laughter: Select Fragments of Greek Comedy*. Oxford: Oxford University Press, 2007.

Orchard, Andy. *A Critical Companion to Beowulf*. London: Boydell and Brewer, 2003.

Orwell, George. *Why I Write*. New York: Penguin Great Ideas, 2005.

O'Toole, L.M., and A. Shukman, eds. *Russian Poetics in Translation*. Translated by O'Toole and Shukman. 10 vols. New York: Amazon Electronic Editions, 2013.

Paglia, Camille. *Sex and Violence, Or Nature and Art*. London: Penguin, 1995.

Pausch, Randy. *The Last Lecture*. New York: Hyperion, 2008.

Peachin, Michael, ed. *The Oxford Handbook of Social Relations in the Roman World*. Oxford: Oxford University Press, 2011.

Pearson, Christine, and Christine Porath. *The Cost of Bad Behavior: How Incivility Is Damaging Your Business and What to Do about It*. New York: Penguin, 2009.

Pink, Daniel. *Drive: The Surprising Truth about What Motivates Us*. New York: Riverhead, 2011.

———. *A Whole New Mind: Why Right Brainers Will Rule the Future*. New York: Riverhead, 2006.

Pinker, Steven. *The Better Angels of Our Nature: Why Violence Has Declined*. New York: Penguin, 2012.

Plato. *The Laws*.

———. *Phaedo*

———. *The Republic,* Books I and X.

———. *The Sophist.*

Ricoeur, Paul. *Freud and Philosophy: An Essay on Interpretation.* Translated by Denis Savage. New Haven: Yale University Press, 1970.

Robinson, Ken. *The Arts in Schools: Principles, Practice, and Provision.* London: Calouste Gulbenkian Foundation, 1982.

———. "Bring on the Learning Revolution!" 2010. www.ted.com/talks/sir_ken_robin son_bring_on_the_revolution

———. *The Element: How Finding Your Passion Changes Everything.* New York: Viking, 2009.

———. *Finding Your Element: How to Discover Your Talents and Passions and Transform Your Life.* New York: Viking, 2013.

———. "How Schools Kill Creativity." 2006. www.ted.com/talks/ken_robinson_says _schools_kill_creativity

———. "How to Escape Education's Death Valley." 2013. www.ted.com/talks/ken_robin son_how_to_escape_education_s_death_valley

Rorty, Richard M. *The Linguistic Turn: Recent Essays in Philosophical Method.* Chicago: University of Chicago Press, 1967.

Rousseau, Jean-Jacques. *Confessions.* Translated by Angela Scholar. Oxford: Oxford University Press, 2008.

Saxonhouse, Arlene. *Free Speech and Democracy in Ancient Athens.* Cambridge: Cambridge University Press, 2006.

Schank, Roger. *Teaching Minds: How Cognitive Science Can Save Our Schools.* New York: Teacher's College Press, 2011.

Scott-Baumann, Alison. *Ricoeur and the Hermeneutics of Suspicion.* London: Continuum, 2011.

Seligman, Martin E.P., and Mihaly Csikszentmihalyi. "Positive Psychology: An Introduction." *American Psychologist* 55, no. 1 (2000): 5–14.

Seneca. *Six Tragedies.* Translated by Emily Wilson. Oxford: Oxford University Press, 2010.

Smiley, Tavis, and Cornel West. *The Rich and the Rest of Us: A Poverty Manifesto.* Washington: Smiley Books, 2012.

Sontag, Susan. *AIDS and Its Metaphors.* New York: Farrar, Straus and Giroux, 1988.

———. *Illness as Metaphor.* New York: Farrar, Straus and Giroux, 1988.

———. *On Photography.* London: Picador, 2001.

———. *Regarding the Pain of Others.* London: Picador, 2004.

Spinoza, Benedict de. *Ethics.* Translated by Edwin Curley. New York: Penguin, 2004.

Veeser, H. Aram, Ed. *The New Historicism.* New York: Routledge, 1989.

Voltaire. *Candide: Or, Optimism.* Translated by Peter Constantine. New York: Modern Library, 2005.

Walter, David. *The Oxford Union: Playground of Power.* London: Macdonald, 1984.

West, Cornel. *Race Matters.* New York: Vintage, 1994.

Wittgenstein, Ludwig. *Tractatus Logico-Philosophicus.* Translated by C.K. Ogden. New York: Routledge, 2004.

Index

academic meetings: potential of as creative community, 82; as urban warfare, 72

academic politics, 95

academy: adaptation in age of IT, 67–69, 80–81; areas of research and teaching, 83; changing role of professors, 66–67; creative/critical balance in, 37–41, 45; creativity, and the Digital Revolution, 7–8; demographics of, 33; "factory model" of, 23–24; funding, and understaffing, 105; hermeneutics of suspicion, 57, 116n4; hierarchical structure of, 4, 14; intellectual combat, tradition of, 4–6, 95; and "know thyself," 13, 101, 111n5; nostalgia, disease of, 38–39; positive psychology courses, 62–63, 116n7; potential of as creative community, 65–66; quality of service, incentivizing, 89; tenure system, 36, 60–61, 108–9; traditional disciplines, decline in, 39, 56–57; university as goal of education, 69. *See also* professors; universities

ad hominem attack, 7, 108; association of ideas with identity, 42–43; character assassination, 28

aggression: aggressive piety of Christianity, 17–18; and critical thinking, 6, 7, 24, 32; and revenge, 12

aggression-based thought, biology of, 27

Amis, Kingsley, 73

Apple, 34, 35

Aquinas, Thomas, 19–20

Aristophanes, 16

Aristotelian logic, 12, 22, 24

Aristotle: creativity, and the arts, 16, 112n10, 112n11; taxonomy of logical presentation, 19; two-part logic, 12

artistic practice, and creativity, 93–95

The Artist's Way (Cameron), 93

arts, conflict with reason, 16

Assange, Julian, 54

assumptions, questioning of, 13

Augustine, Saint, *City of God*, 19

Beowulf, 20, 112–13n18

Bolinda Introduction to Critical Thinking, xii

Bourdieu, Pierre, 49; *habitus*, 97

brainstorming: as creative sharing, 33–34; role of criticism in, 37

Buddhism, and Eastern critical thought, 13

Buffet, Warren, 55–56

bullies, 96

business: creative work, and innovation, 55–56; desire for creative skills, 7; incentives, and productive collaboration, 96; interest in contributory thinking, 3; and over-education, 99–100, 101; philanthropy, 55–56

business faculties, enrolment in, 39

125